Sew Any Set-in Pocket

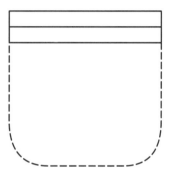

Copyright ©1994 Claire B. Shaeffer

Published in Radnor, Pennsylvania 19089, by
Chilton Book Company

Manufactured in the United States of America

A CIP record for this book is available from the
Library of Congress.

ISBN 0-8019-8399-1

1 2 3 4 5 6 7 8 9 0   3 2 1 0 9 8 7 6 5 4

Design: Martha Vercoutere
Editors: Robbie Fanning, Rosalie Cooke
Production: Kendra Armer, Gil Bowers
Technical Illustration: Pamela S. Poole
Fashion Illustration: Deva
Seamstress: Pat Whittemore
Computer Assistance: Kali Fanning Murrell and
                            Jonathan Murrell

Are you interested in a quarterly newsletter
about creative uses of the sewing machine,
serger, and knitting machine? Write to:

The Creative Machine,
PO Box 2634-B,
Menlo Park, CA 94026-2634.

Special thanks for pocket tips to:

Naomi Baker
Gail Brown
Clotilde
Miss Adeline Giuntini
Margaret Komives
Elizabeth Lawson
Donna Salyers
Jan Saunders
Marcy Tilton
Jane Whiteley
Tammy Young
Nancy Zieman

to Janet Lewis
for editorial assistance

and to the staffs at Open Chain
and Chilton for their expertise
and enthusiasm

Other Books by Claire Shaeffer:

Claire Shaeffer's Fabric Sewing Guide. Radnor,
PA: Chilton Book Co., 1989. (All Claire
Shaeffer books are available from Box 157,
Palm Springs, CA 92263.)

Claire Shaeffer's Sewing S.O.S. Menlo Park, CA:
Open Chain Publishing, 1988.

The Complete Book of Sewing Short Cuts. New
York: Sterling Publishing Co., Inc., 1981.

Couture Sewing Techniques. Newtown, CT:
The Taunton Press, 1994.

Price It Right. Palm Springs, CA: Claire
Shaeffer.

Sew A Beatiful Gift. New York: Sterling Publishing Co., Inc.

Sew Any Patch Pocket. Menlo Park, CA: Open
Chain Publishing, Inc., 1992.

Sew Any Set-in Pocket

Claire B. Shaeffer

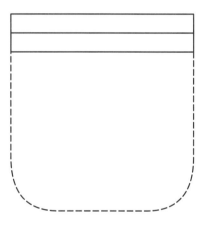

Chilton Book Company
Radnor, Pennsylvania

Contents

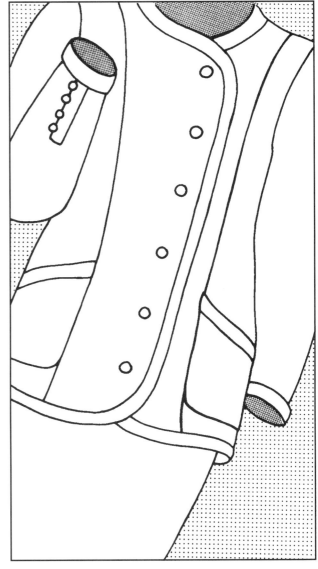

Other Books Available From Chilton

Robbie Fanning, Series Editor

Contemporary Quilting Series

Appliqué the Ann Boyce Way, by Ann Boyce
Contemporary Quilting Techniques, by Pat Cairns
Fast Patch, by Anita Hallock
Fourteen Easy Baby Quilts, by Margaret Dittman
Machine-Quilted Jackets, Vests, and Coats, by Nancy Moore
Pictorial Quilts, by Carolyn Hall
Precision-Pieced Quilts Using the Foundation Method, by Jane Hall and Dixie Haywood
Quick Quilted Home Decor With Your Sewing Machine, by Jackie Dodson
The Quilter's Guide to Rotary Cutting, by Donna Poster
Quilts by the Slice, by Beckie Olson
Scrap Quilts Using Fast Patch, by Anita Hallock
Speed-Cut Quilts, by Donna Poster
Super Simple Quilts, by Kathleen Eaton
Teach Yourself Machine Piecing and Quilting, by Debra Wagner
Three-Dimensional Appliqué, by Jodie Davis

Creative Machine Arts Series

ABCs of Serging, by Tammy Young and Lori Bottom
The Button Lover's Book, by Marilyn Green
Claire Shaeffer's Fabric Sewing Guide
The Complete Book of Machine Embroidery, by Robbie and Tony Fanning
Creative Nurseries Illustrated, by Debra Terry and Juli Plooster
Creative Serging Illustrated, The New, by Pati Palmer, Gail Brown, and Sue Green
Distinctive Serger Gifts and Crafts, by Naomi Baker and Tammy Young
The Fabric Lover's Scrapbook, by Margaret Dittman
Friendship Quilts by Hand and Machine, by Carolyn Vosburg Hall
Gifts Galore, by Jane Warnick and Jackie Dodson
How to Make Soft Jewelry, by Jackie Dodson
Innovative Serging, by Gail Brown and Tammy Young
Innovative Sewing, by Gail Brown and Tammy Young
Owner's Guide to Sewing Machines, Sergers, and Knitting Machines, by Gale Grigg Hazen
Petite Pizzazz, by Barb Griffin
Putting on the Glitz, by Sandra L. Hatch and Ann Boyce
Second Stitches, by Susan D. Parker
Serge a Simple Project, by Tammy Young and Naomi Baker
Serged Garments in Minutes, by Tammy Young and Naomi Baker
Sew Sensational Gifts, by Naomi Baker and Tammy Young
Sew, Serge, Press, by Jan Saunders
Sewing and Collecting Vintage Fashions, by Eileen MacIntosh
Simply Serge Any Fabric, by Naomi Baker and Tammy Young
Soft Gardens, by Yvonne Perez-Collins
Twenty Easy Machine-Made Rugs, by Jackie Dodson

Open Chain Books

Gail Brown's All-New Instant Interiors, by Gail Brown
Jane Asher's Costume Book, by Gail Brown
Learn Bearmaking, by Judi Maddigan
Quick Napkin Creations, by Gail Brown
Sew Any Patch Pocket, by Claire Shaeffer
Singer Instructions for Art Embroidery and Lace Work
Soft Toys for Babies, by Judi Maddigan

Crafts Kaleidoscope

Fabric Painting Made Easy, by Nancy Ward
How to Make Cloth Books for Children, by Anne Pellowski
Quick and Easy Ways With Ribbon, by Ceci Johnson
Too Hot to Handle?/Potholders and How to Make Them, by Doris Hoover

StarWear

Embellishments, by Linda Fry Kenzle
Sweatshirts With Style, by Mary Mulari

Know Your Sewing Machine Series, by Jackie Dodson

Know Your Bernina, second edition
Know Your Brother, with Jane Warnick
Know Your Elna, with Carol Ahles
Know Your New Home, with Judi Cull and Vicki Lynn Hastings
Know Your Pfaff, with Audrey Griese
Know Your Sewing Machine
Know Your Singer
Know Your Viking, with Jan Saunders
Know Your White, with Jan Saunders

Know Your Serger Series, by Tammy Young and Naomi Baker

Know Your baby lock
Know Your Pfaff Hobbylock
Know Your Serger
Know Your White Superlock

Teach Yourself to Sew Better Series, by Jan Saunders

A Step-by-Step Guide to Your Bernina
A Step-by-Step Guide to Your New Home
A Step-by-Step Guide to Your Sewing Machine
A Step-by-Step Guide to Your Viking

Introduction

Set-in or bag pockets have the pocket sack on the inside of the garment with only the opening visible on the outside, unlike patch pockets, which have large, visible pouches on the outside of the garment. Set-in pockets can be used on all types of garments and fabrics, for children and adults, but they are generally dressier than patch pockets and they do not withstand as much abuse.

Many set-in pockets are described by their openings—inseam, edge, porthole, double-welt, welt, flap—but they all fall into two broad categories: **inseam pockets**, which are set into seamlines or darts, and **slash pockets**, which are set into a slash on the body of the garment. Generally inseam pockets are considered easier to sew, while slashed pockets are considered more difficult. Actually, neither is really difficult, but if you want professional results, *precision at every step—marking, stitching, cutting, and pressing—is a must*.

When designing pockets, study current trends and examine the pockets on ready-made garments, as well as in photographs in catalogs and magazines. You'll find a treasure chest of ideas.

Pockets can be used singly, in pairs, or in multiples, but usually single pockets are easier to place attractively than multiples.

The pocket size should be appropriate for the size of the wearer and/or the garment, but the size is also influenced by the garment style, pocket location, fabric choice, and current fashion trends.

One of the easiest ways to design with pockets is to substitute one type pocket for another. Since many of today's patterns feature patch pockets, you can immediately add a more expensive look by replacing the patch pockets with slash pockets.

How to Use This Book

1. This book is divided into two main parts, Part I: Inseam Pockets and Part II: Slash Pockets. Each part includes many variations and design ideas. Additional information for Welts and Flaps is in the Appendix. Read How to Design a Set-in Pocket, then review Pocket Terminology. These terms are important to understanding the techniques presented in this book. Next, read Pattern Development and Sewing Notes, both for your design and for the basic design.

2. Choose a pocket to make. It can be on a commercial pattern, an original design, or a copy of a ready-made design in a magazine or store window that appeals to you.

3. Look through the illustrations in this book. Find a design that matches your idea closely.

4. Analyze the pocket, comparing it to the illustrated design. Is it set into a seam? Is it in a slash? Does it have welts or flaps? Does it have a novelty feature like an unusual opening or a special treatment of patterned fabric?

5. Now make a sample. Remember that all directions assume you have already read about the Basic Pocket that is at the beginning of each part. If you need to refresh your memory when the directions say "Make the pocket sacks" or "Complete the pocket," turn back to that Basic Pocket. If the pocket has flaps and welts, also refer to the Appendix. Practice until you are pleased with the results. Save your samples as references for the next time you make that pocket.

6. Share what you've learned. Show others your pocket samples. Improve your own skills by teaching a friend. Pockets are an easy, fast way to develop new skills and perfect old ones.

Pocket Terminology

All-in-one pocket 1) inseam pocket cut in one piece with the garment section; 2) pocket sack cut with the underpocket and upper pocket in one piece; 3) welt pocket cut with the welt and upper pocket in one piece.

Applied welt pocket separate welt applied to the garment section, sometimes called outside or tailored welt, upright or upturned flap, stand, breast, or handkerchief pocket.

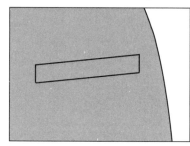

Besom-welt pocket 1) slashed pocket with a wide welt at the bottom and a narrow welt at the top; 2) sometimes used to describe any double-welt pocket.

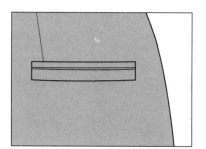

Closed inseam pocket or **closed seam pocket** utilitarian pocket inserted inconspicuously into a seam between two garment sections. Sometimes called basic seam pocket, seam pocket, or side seam pocket, but generally referred to as an inseam or side pocket. See inseam pocket.

Double-welt pocket a slash pocket with two welts at the opening. Known by a variety of names such as bound, piped, slashed, double-bound, double lip, buttonhole, tailored, besom, hacking, and jetted pockets, it resembles a large bound buttonhole.

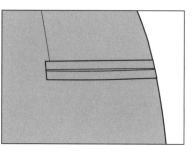

Edge pocket decorative inseam pocket located at the edge of a garment section. Sometimes called structural, stylized, or open seam pocket.

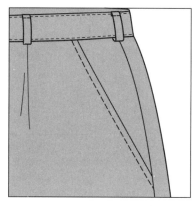

Extension portion of the garment section which extends into the pocket beyond the seamline, sometimes called the pocket hem.

Flap small, flat garment section attached only at the top, used with or instead of a pocket.

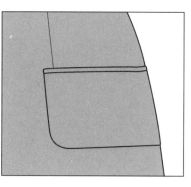

Flap pocket a slash pocket with a flap. When used with double welts, flap can be inserted between the welts or between the upper welt and garment section.

Inseam pocket 1) any pocket set into a seamline; 2) frequently used to describe the closed inseam or side pocket.

Mouthline the opening between the welts, sometimes called the mouth.

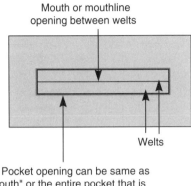

Mouth or mouthline opening between welts

Welts

Pocket opening can be same as "mouth" or the entire pocket that is seen on outside of garment (outlined).

Placement line same as mouthline.

Pocket facing 1) self-fabric section of pocket sack that is applied or seamed to lining sack; 2) another name for upper pocket because it faces the bottom of the opening. It can be cut from self-fabric, lining material, or pocketing fabric.

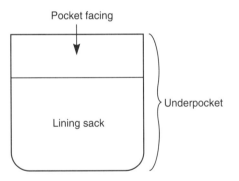

Pocket facing

Underpocket

Lining sack

Pocket opening 1) portion of set-in pocket visible on outside of garment; 2) the mouthline or placement line.

Pocket placement line location for mouthline.

Pocket sack, bag, pouch the portion of the pocket on the inside of the garment. It can be one piece, made of self-fabric or lining, or it can be two pieces with a pocket facing applied to the pocket sack or seamed to it.

Pocketing fabric tightly woven cotton twill material that is very durable, available in different weights, used on men's trousers.

Set-in pocket any pocket set into a seam between two garment sections or into a slash on a garment section.

Styleline the pocket opening. Although it is usually a straight line, it can be curved.

Tab small flap or loop with a buttonhole or snap used to close a pocket.

Slash pocket any pocket set into a slash on a garment section.

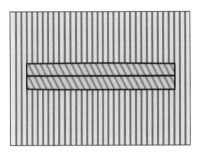

Tailored pocket any pocket used on the face side of a tailored garment, regardless of its style or position.

Underlay on edge pockets, the underpocket and the portion of the garment section that shows above or to the side of the pocket.

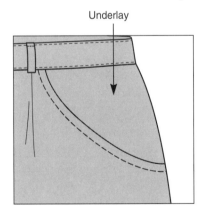

Underlay

Underpocket the pocket sack nearest the body, sometimes called back pocket.

Underpocket facing self-fabric facing used on inseam and slashed pockets to hide the lining fabric when the pocket is used. It can be applied to the top of the underpocket or cut separately and seamed to the top edge of the underpocket.

Underpocket sack lining fabric section of the underpocket, sometimes cut using the underpocket pattern and sometimes cut smaller and seamed to the underpocket facing.

Upper pocket the pocket sack which finishes the lower edge of the pocket opening and is nearest the outside of the garment, sometimes called top pocket or the pocket facing (because it is the facing of the opening edge).

Upper pocket facing used on men's garments and expensive ladies' designs, a self-fabric facing at the top of the upper pocket when the lower pocket is made of lining fabric. Upper pocket facing can be applied on top of the lining fabric or they can be seamed together.

Upper pocket sack seamed to an upper pocket facing to reduce bulk on the upper pocket.

Welt 1) narrow band of fabric that stands up on the lower edge of the pocket opening, sometimes called a stand; 2) one of two narrow bands of fabric on both edges of the pocket opening, sometimes called binding, piping, or lip. See drawing for mouthline.

How to Design A Set-in Pocket

1. Make a rough sketch or copy a photograph from your file of pocket ideas. Make several photocopies and experiment with possible ideas.

2. Draw the pocket on the garment pattern. Position and draw it exactly the same size and shape as it will be on the finished garment. Use short dashes or a colored pencil to indicate the pocket sack on the inside of the garment.

Hint: *If you're using a commercial pattern that has a patch pocket instead of a set-in pocket, use the opening on the patch pocket as a guide for placing the pocket.*

3. If you're not making a test garment (toile), "try on" the paper pattern to see if the pocket size, shape, and location are appropriate to your design and figure. Or compare the pocket placement and size to similar designs in your wardrobe, your pattern collection, or current fashions.

4. Make the pocket on pattern paper.

Hint: *I use physician's examining paper, available from medical supply houses (see the Yellow Pages), but wax paper, butcher paper, and pattern cloth are also good choices. If you can't see through the pattern paper, place the original pattern on top and trace with a stiletto tracing wheel.*

Part I:

Inseam Pockets

All inseam pockets are located in the seamlines of the garment and run the gamut from pockets which are very practical and inconspicuous to pockets which are more decorative than useful. But no matter how diverse, all fall into two categories: **inseam pockets**, which are hidden in traditional seamlines, and **edge pockets**, which are conspicuous and formed when the edge of one garment section is set against another section.

More practical than ornamental, inseam pockets are frequently located in the side seams of skirts, pants, jackets, and coats. They can be added to ready-made garments or removed without compromising the aesthetics of the design. By contrast, edge pockets are more pronounced and frequently an important element of the design. And when they are removed (by sewing the seam without a pocket), the integrity of the design can easily be affected.

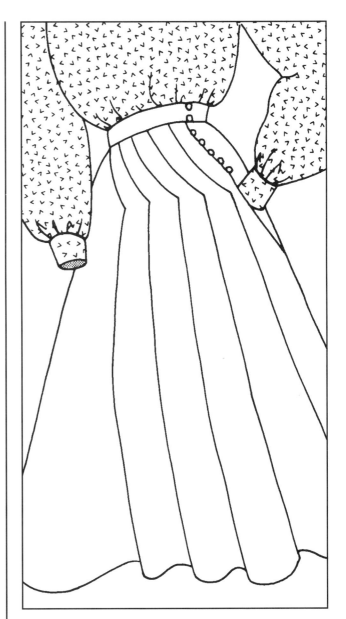

Standards for Inseam Pockets

1. Make pockets inconspicuous, unless they are designed to be decorative.

2. Position functional pockets so they're convenient to use.

3. Make openings large enough that the pocket can be used easily. Generally, openings should be large enough for the hand to be inserted without difficulty; however, a few pockets, such as watch and ticket pockets, are always very small.

4. Pockets should be smooth and firm at the opening so the seamline appears continuous. Check that both edges are the same length, unless designed otherwise.

5. The opening should not gap and the underpocket should not show. Make the underpocket of self-fabric, use a self-fabric facing at the edge, or add an extension on the garment section that extends into the pocket if the underpocket will show while sitting or moving.

6. Reinforce the pocket opening so it won't stretch out of shape.

7. Don't let thread ends at pocket openings and seamlines show on the right side.

8. Secure pocket openings with backtacks or knots so they won't rip out. If the pockets will be used extensively, reinforce the ends of the openings so they won't tear.

9. Make any topstitching appear continuous without bald spots or overlapping.

10. Welts and flaps used with inseam pockets should meet the standards of Welts and Flaps (see Appendix page 107).

11. Construct pocket sacks of bulk-free, durable fabrics with the same care requirements as the fashion fabric. They should be invisible or at least inconspicuous from the right side of the garment. The seam around the pocket sack should lie flat without pulling or puckering. Finish raw edges appropriately.

12. Design the depth of the pocket to be appropriate for the pocket location and use. Don't make it so shallow that items fall out or so deep that the pocket sack extends into the hem, the facing area, or beyond the edge of the garment, or hangs below the finger tips.

13. Sew the top of the pocket sack into a horizontal seam when possible to avoid sagging and distortion of the seamline.

Sidebar

12 Topstitching Tips

1. Clean and oil the machine (if appropriate) before beginning.

2. Insert a new needle, the smallest possible.

3. Check to be sure there is enough thread on the spool and bobbin.

4. Experiment on sample seams made from fabric scraps. Use a topstitching foot if you have one. If not, try stitching with a zipper foot to the right of the needle. It rides over the seam, one edge touching the seamline. If drag lines are a problem, experiment with an even-feed foot, walking foot, or roller foot.

5. Stitch with the garment right side up.

6. Stitch both side seams in the same direction.

7. If the fabric has a nap, stitch in the direction of the nap.

8. Stitch slowly at an even speed.

9. Hold the garment firmly in front and back of the presser foot when stitching.

10. If skipped stitches are a problem, use a needle lubricant on the spool thread, tension discs, and needle.

11. If you have only 5" or 6" more to topstitch and you run out of thread, tie the thread end to the thread on a new spool and continue stitching. You should be able to finish before the knot reaches the eye of the needle.

12. If you run out of thread in the middle of a line of topstitching, resume stitching by inserting the machine needle precisely into the last hole stitched. When you finish, pull the thread ends to the wrong side and knot them.

1. Inseam Pockets

The inseam pocket is known by many names—inseam pocket, closed inseam pocket, closed seam pocket, side pocket, side seam pocket, and basic inseam pocket. It is the foundation for many variations and can be located in yoke seams on blouses and skirts; in the side-front seams of skirts, pants, princess-line dresses, and jackets; in waistline seams on skirts and slacks; in decorative seams; in darts; and, of course, in side seams.

The Basic Inseam Pocket is the most popular style. Inconspicuous and easy to sew, it is used more frequently on women's designs than on men's, and it's generally a better choice for larger figures than are other pocket styles.

The basic inseam pocket is almost invisible when sewn and fitted properly. And even though it works best when the garment has sufficient fullness to hide the pocket underneath, it can be added to most patterns and even to ready-made garments (see page 11). In fact, when side pockets are omitted or removed and the garment sections sewn together, there is little, if any, effect on the garment design and fit.

All basic inseam pockets look more or less the same from outside of the garment. But on the inside, depending on the number and shape of the pattern pieces, there are three different pocket styles: 1. the Basic Inseam Pocket, 2. the Inseam Pocket with an Extension, and 3. the All-in-One Inseam Pocket.

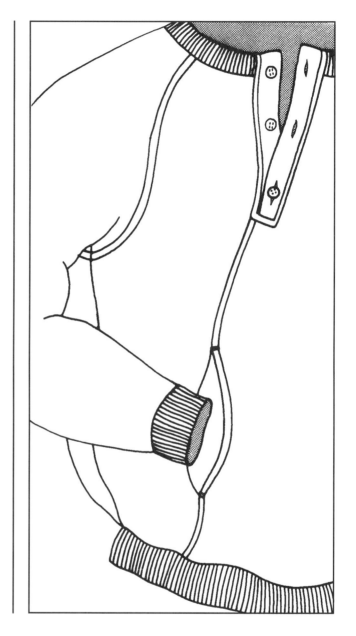

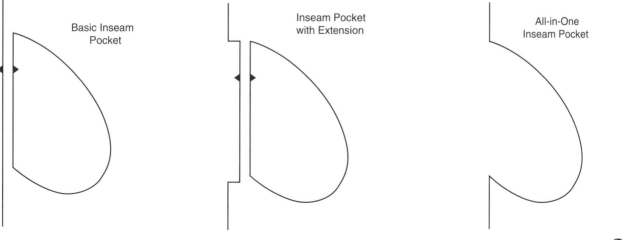

Basic Inseam Pocket

Inseam Pocket with Extension

All-in-One Inseam Pocket

None of these pockets is universally best, but generally, pockets with extensions and all-in-one pockets are more attractive and less conspicuous than the Basic Inseam Pocket. Since you are the designer, you can use one type of pocket for the upper pocket and another for the underpocket. The choice will depend on the garment design, amount of time available, the fabric weight, and maybe your budget.

Pattern Development for Basic Inseam Pocket

The foundation of all inseam pockets, these directions for the Basic Inseam or Closed Seam Pocket can be adapted for any variation. They can be used on original patterns or with commercial patterns which do not have inseam pockets.

1. Plan the pocket on the garment front pattern.

Draw the pocket opening 6" to 7" wide and locate it on the seamline 1" to 2" below the waistline. (See Inseam Pocket Pattern in Appendix.)

Hint: *I draw the pocket shape on the wrong side of the pattern, like the pocket will lie against the body under the fashion fabric.*

2. Using short dashes or a colored pencil, draw the pocket sack 5" to 6-1/2" wide and so that it extends 3" to 5" below the opening.

Indicate a matchpoint somewhere on the opening seamline and two matchpoints on the sack seamline.

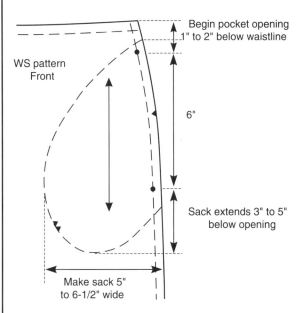

Begin pocket opening 1" to 2" below waistline

WS pattern Front

6"

Sack extends 3" to 5" below opening

Make sack 5" to 6-1/2" wide

Establish the grainline parallel to the garment's grainline.

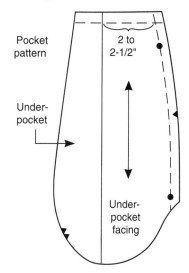

Hints: If the garment has a waistline or horizontal seam, pockets below the waist hang better when the top of the sack is caught in the seamline. To shape the top of the pocket, use the cutting line on the garment waistline as a guide.

To reduce bulk, shape the pocket below the opening so that it isn't caught in the side seam.

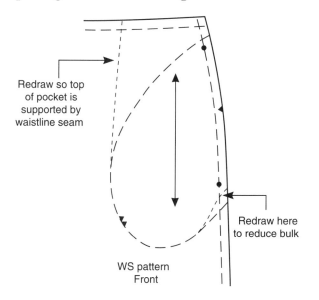

Redraw so top of pocket is supported by waistline seam

Redraw here to reduce bulk

WS pattern Front

3. Trace the new pattern, the grainline, and matchpoints on a piece of pattern paper. Add seam allowances as needed on the new pattern. Mark the pocket pattern "Cut 2"—one for the underpocket and one for the upper pocket.

Hint: When working with commercial patterns, I trace the cutting lines wherever possible instead of the seamlines so that I don't have to add seam allowances.

4. Optional underpocket facing: If the underpocket will be cut from lining fabric, make an underpocket facing to cover the lining so it won't show at the opening when you sit or move.

Begin by drawing the facing on the pocket pattern. Draw a line 2" to 2-1/2" from the side seam and parallel to the grainline. Establish the grainline parallel to the pocket on the underpocket facing.

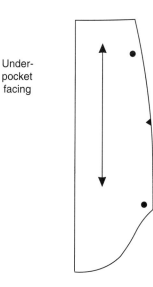

Pocket pattern

2 to 2-1/2"

Under-pocket

Under-pocket facing

On a separate piece of paper, trace and mark the cutting lines and grainline for the new underpocket facing pattern.

Under-pocket facing

A. Basic Inseam Pocket

Design Analysis:

The basic inseam pocket has two separate pocket sacks sewn to the regular garment seam allowance. It can easily be added to any pattern, even to ready-made garments. It can be used on most fabrics and sewn by a variety of methods, and because it's a basic design, it can be used as a foundation for many variations. It requires the least amount of fashion fabric and is generally least expensive to sew. But a word of caution: if the pocket gaps and the pocket sacks are made from lining materials, the lining will show when you sit and move, making the garment look cheap.

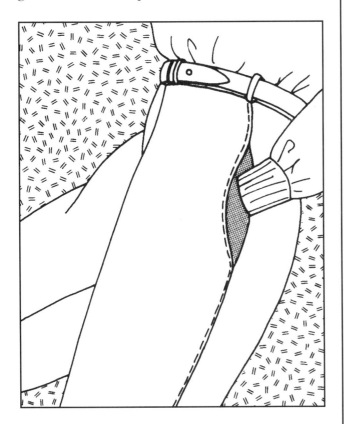

Construction Analysis:

In the Basic method, the pocket sacks are first joined to the garment sections, then the side seams above and below the pocket are stitched and pressed open, and finally the pocket sack is stitched.

Sewing Notes:

In these general directions, the popular side seam pocket is used to illustrate the Basic Inseam Pocket. The principles apply to most inseam pockets including many edge pockets. Special techniques for specific designs and variations are found in the following chapters.

Hint: For professional results, all inseam pockets must be marked, stitched, cut, and pressed precisely.

1. Cut out the garment and pocket sacks.

Hint: When sewing garments made of transparent and light-colored fabrics, cut the pocket sacks from flesh-colored or light brown fabric so the pocket sacks will be less conspicuous.

2. Mark the pocket opening on the wrong side of the garment and pocket sections with a temporary marking pen, chalk, chalk wheel, soap sliver, thread tracing, dressmaker's carbon, or short clips.

3. Reinforce the opening with a stay appropriate to the garment quality and fabric weave so the opening won't stretch out of shape and the fabric won't tear at the top and bottom of the opening. If the opening is on the lengthwise grain or crossgrain and the pocket won't be used extensively, reinforce only the front of the opening.

Suitable stay materials include 1/2"-wide strips of lightweight fusible interfacing, 1/4"-wide strips of lightweight selvage, or woven seam binding. Fuse, machine stitch, or hand sew the stay in place.

Hint: An advantage of a fusible stay is that it can also be used to reinforce the top and bottom of the pocket opening when the fabric is loosely woven or if the pocket will be used extensively.

Cut the stay 2" longer than the opening then mark the opening length in the center of the stay.

When *fusing or machine stitching the stay,* position it so one edge is aligned with the seamline and the bulk of the stay is on the seam allowance.

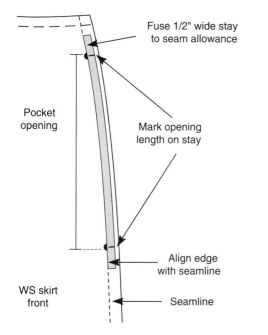

When *hand sewing the stay,* use a narrow strip of lightweight selvage. Center the stay over the seamline and secure it with a short running stitch. Work carefully so the stitches won't show on the right side.

4. If the underpocket has a self-fabric facing, cut the inside edge with a selvage or finish the edge of the facing that will extend into the pocket in this way:

On *lightweight cottons, polyesters,* and *silks,* clean finish the edge.

On *bulky* or *heavy fabrics,* finish the edge with a multi-stitch zigzag, regular zigzag, serged edge, or seam tape.

Right sides up, align the opening edges of the underpocket and its facing. Pin and stitch 1/4" from the edge. Smooth and pin the facing over the underpocket. Edgestitch the remaining long edge flat against the underpocket. Press.

5. Right sides together, match and pin the upper pocket to the garment front. Stitch. Repeat for the underpocket and garment back.

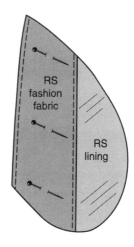

Underpocket with fashion fabric facing

Hint: *To position the seamline just inside the pocket, stitch using a 1/4" seam allowance instead of the usual 5/8". This will reposition the seamline inside the pocket instead of at the opening.*

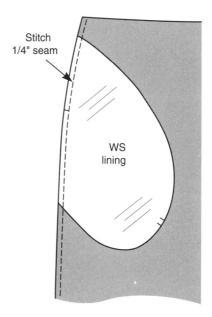

6. With the garment front wrong side up, press. On the garment front, press the pocket seam toward the pocket.

Hint: *For a sharper edge or seamline, first press the seam flat; then press it open.*

7. Understitch the seamline, trim, finish the raw edges of the seam as needed, and press. Repeat on the garment back.

Hints: *When understitching, begin with the pocket right side up, stitch through the upper pocket and both layers of the seam. Use the inside of the straight-stitch presser foot as a guide to stitch close (1/16") to the seamline.*

When pressing the pocket opening, begin wrong sides together with the pocket uppermost. Roll the seamline toward the pocket and press the edge.

8. Right sides together, match the raw edges and notches of the garment sections. Pin or baste the pocket opening closed. Stitch the garment above and below the opening. Back-stitch, spottack, or tie knots to secure the thread ends at the opening.

Hints: *Elizabeth Lawson uses a piece of transparent tape to ensure precision. Place the edge of the tape on the seamline and mark the ends of the opening on it.*

When tying knots, pull both threads to one side. Give the threads a sharp tug first. Then tie the two ends together with a tailor's (overhand) knot set close to the fabric.

9. Topstitch the opening if desired. Pin each pocket sack flat against its garment section. Turn the garment over. From the right side, topstitch the garment front opening. Beginning at the top of the opening, stitch forward 1/4" in, then reverse 1/4", and stitch forward again 1/4". Pivot and stitch parallel to edge of the opening. At the bottom, stitch to the opening, reverse, and stitch back. Remove the pins and press.

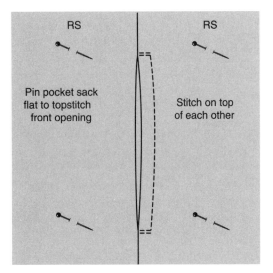

RS   RS

Pin pocket sack flat to topstitch front opening

Stitch on top of each other

When used on designs made of denim, synthetic suedes, or leather which have topstitched seamlines, place the row of top-stitching the desired distance from the opening and parallel to it. Do not stitch across the top and bottom or above and below the opening. Pull the thread ends to the underside and knot.

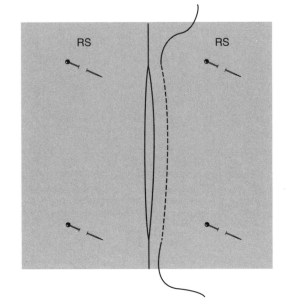

RS   RS

Hint: *To avoid a gap at the ends of the opening when topstitching, begin stitching at the ends of the opening. Use a foot like a straight stitch zipper foot or jeans foot that allows you to see the end of the stitched line so you can begin and end precisely. If there is still a little gap at the ends, pull the thread ends into a self-threading or calyx-eyed needle and take an extra hand stitch to cover the gap. Leave long threads so you can pull them to the underside and knot.*

10. With the wrong side up, press the seam flat, then press the pocket toward the front. Clip the back seam allowance as needed to the ends of the opening so the seam allowance will lie flat. Press the side seam open below the pocket.

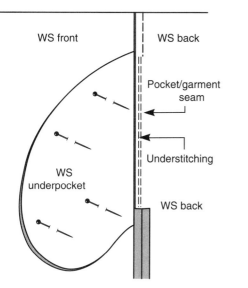

11. Smooth the pocket sections toward the front and pin them together. Stitch around the pocket, beginning and ending at the ends of the opening. Backtack.

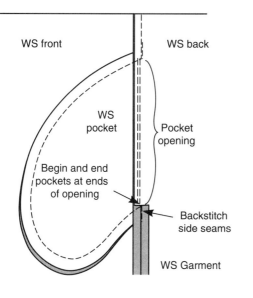

Hint: *When the pocket sections are smoothed and pinned, the raw edges may not match perfectly. If the edges don't match, there's no problem, but the pockets must be smooth, or the garment won't hang properly.*

12. On the garment side seams, finish the seam allowances separately. On the pocket, finish the edges together. Press.

13. If you didn't topstitch the opening earlier, it's more difficult now, but it can still be done. First topstitch above and below the opening, stopping precisely at the opening and leaving long threads ends. Then, using a free-arm machine, topstitch the pocket opening. Again, stop precisely at the opening, leaving long threads. Pull the threads to the underside, knot, and trim.

Hints: *I sometimes take an extra stitch into the opening to be sure I don't have a bald spot—the extra stitch isn't hard to unpick if I don't need it.*

Use a calyx-eyed or self-threading needle to pull the threads through quickly and easily.

Variation: Sonia Rykiel Pocket

Design Analysis:

Used on a pair of expensive wool jersey pants designed by Sonia Rykiel, this novelty inseam pocket is an easy variation of the Basic Side Pocket. The pull-on pants had decorative wrong-side-out serged seams.

First, the garment front and upper pocket are joined in the usual manner with right sides together. The pocket sack is stitched, then the garment is assembled wrong sides together.

Sewing Notes:

1. Cut the underpocket from self-fabric and the upper pocket from lining fabric.

2. Mark the pocket opening and reinforce as needed.

3. Right sides together, pin the upper pocket and garment front together. Stitch the opening with a 5/8" seam. Begin and end precisely at the ends of the opening with a backstitch. Press.

4. Clip both front and pocket seam allowances to the ends of the stitched line. Understitch, trim, and press.

5. Turn the pocket to the wrong side.

6. Right side up, lay the underpocket flat on the table. Cover it with the front garment section which is also right side up. Fold the front back so you can match and pin the pocket sacks together. Stitch around the pocket sack. Begin and end at the pocket opening with a backstitch. Serge around the pocket sack.

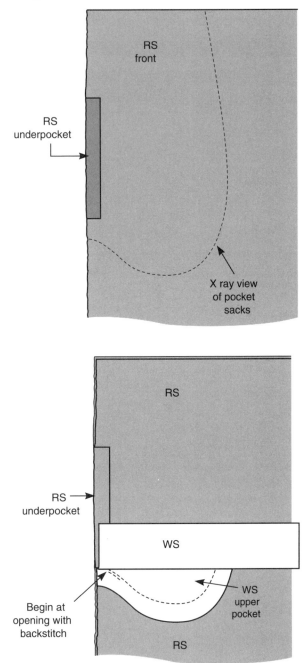

7. Wrong sides together, join the garment front and back by serging on the seamline, letting the serger trim away the excess seam allowances.

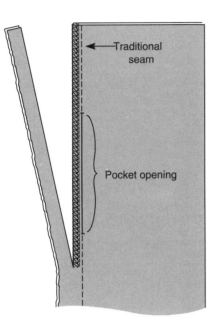

Hints: *If your serger doesn't make a safety stitch, join the front and back with a straight stitch before serging.*

To secure the serged ends, dab the end with a fray retardant, tie them, or use a crochet or latch hook to pull them back through the last 1/2".

Traditional seam

Pocket opening

8. Press the seam flat.

Sidebar

Adding an inseam pocket to ready-to-wear

One of the advantages of the basic inseam pocket is that it can be added easily to the side seams of a ready-made design.

1. Begin by marking the pocket opening locations. Generally pocket openings begin 1" to 2" below the waistline and are about 6" long. To fine tune the positioning more accurately, you can use a similar garment in your wardrobe as a guide or you can try on the garment and mark the locations while it's on the figure.

2. From the wrong side, carefully mark the pocket opening on the seamline. Before ripping the seam in the opening, machine stitch along the seamline for about 1" on either end of the opening with a backstitch at the opening. Then rip out the original seam at the opening.

3. Choose a lightweight lining or interfacing fabric such as Sewin' Sheer, Poly Supreme, China silk, or tricot in a color that matches or coordinates with the garment. For each pocket, cut two pocket sacks from the lining fabric, using the pattern on page 116.

Hint: *When adding pockets to a white garment, cut the sacks from light brown fabric so they will be inconspicuous.*

4. With the garment wrong side up, pin one pocket sack to the garment back, right sides together. Stitch a 1/4" seam. Repeat on the garment front.

5. Complete the pocket using the directions for the basic side pocket on page 6.

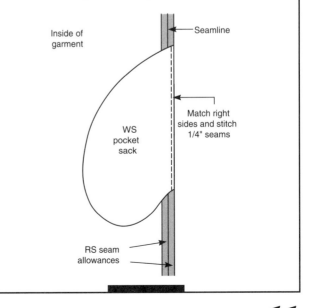

Inside of garment

Seamline

Match right sides and stitch 1/4" seams

WS pocket sack

RS seam allowances

B. Inseam Pocket With Extension

Design Analysis:

A favorite of pattern companies and fashion manufacturers, the inseam pocket with an extension also has separate pocket sacks, but the garment sections extend into the pocket opening so that the seamline which joins the pocket and garment is hidden inside the pocket. It isn't difficult or time-consuming to make, can be used on most fabrics, and looks attractive from the right side. It doesn't require a separate facing for the underpocket back, rarely requires additional fabric, and adds little extra bulk. Unfortunately, you cannot add this kind of pocket to an existing garment.

The pocket sacks are usually cut from lining materials, but they can be made of self-fabric if it's lightweight.

Pattern Development:

1. Review the Pattern Development for the Basic Inseam Pocket on page 4 and make the pocket pattern.

2. On the pocket pattern, draw the extension seamline within the sack shape, 1" to 1-1/2" from the original garment/pocket seamline and parallel to it. Indicate a new matchpoint.

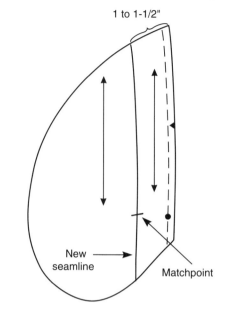

1 to 1-1/2"

New seamline

Matchpoint

Cut the pattern apart on the new seamline, and add seam allowances to each section.

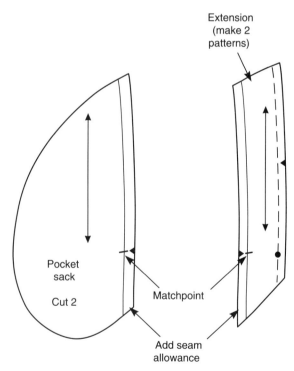

Extension (make 2 patterns)

Pocket sack

Cut 2

Matchpoint

Add seam allowance

On a separate piece of paper, trace the pocket sack and label it "Cut 2."

Trace an extension for the garment back and another for the garment front.

3. Match and pin the seamlines of one pocket extension to the garment back pattern. Repeat for the front pattern.

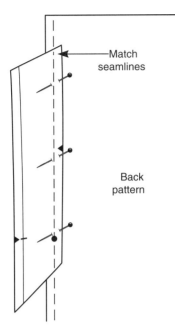

Match seamlines

Back pattern

4. Trace the new pattern sections.

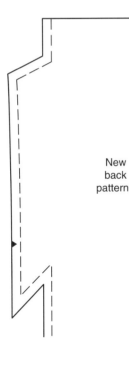

New back pattern

Sewing Notes:

1. Review the Sewing Notes for the Basic Inseam Pocket (see page 6).

2. Mark the pocket opening and reinforce as needed.

> *Hint: I fuse a 1/2"-wide strip of light weight fusible on the underside of the extension aligning the edge of the fusible with the pocket opening.*

3. Right sides together, join the pocket and corresponding garment section. Press the seams toward the pocket, trim to 1/4", and understitch.

> *Hint: To reduce bulk, trim away small triangles at each end of the seam before understitching.*

4. Right sides together, pin the garment sections together. Pin or baste the pocket opening closed. Smooth the pocket toward the garment front, and pin the edges together. Stitch the seam to the opening. Pivot and stitch around the pocket. Pivot again and stitch the remainder of the seam.

> *Hint: To reinforce the ends of the opening, use 1" squares of lightweight interfacing. Stitching with the garment front uppermost, stop about 1/2" from each end of the opening. Slip the square under the fabric layers and continue stitching.*

5. Press the pocket toward the garment front.

6. Press the side seams open. Clip the back seam allowances at the ends of the opening, as needed, so they will lie flat.

7. Finish the raw edges of the seams.

C. All-in-One Inseam Pocket

Design Analysis:

This is the quickest, easiest pocket to sew. It's also the cleanest, since it doesn't have pocket/garment seamlines on the inside of the garment, but it may be too heavy or bulky on some fabrics. If the opening isn't on the straight grain, the pocket sacks won't duplicate the grain of the garment sections. This may affect the drape of the design. On most designs, the fabric waste is considerable, and because of the cost of materials, it's rarely used on ready-made garments.

Hint: If you are using a pattern with an all-in-one inseam pocket and you don't have enough fabric, add a seam so you can cut the pocket sacks separately.

Pattern Development:

1. Review the Pattern Development for the Basic Inseam Pocket on page 4. Make the pocket pattern and a copy.

2. Match and pin the seamlines of one pocket sack pattern and the garment back pattern. Repeat for the front pattern.

3. Trace the new pattern, ignoring the pinned pocket/garment seamline.

Sewing Notes:

1. Review the Sewing Notes for the Basic Inseam Pocket (see page 6).

2. Mark the pocket opening and reinforce as needed.

3. Right sides together, match and pin the front and back garment sections together. Pin or baste the pocket opening closed. Stitch the side seam to the opening. Pivot and stitch around the pocket. Pivot again and stitch the remainder of the seam.

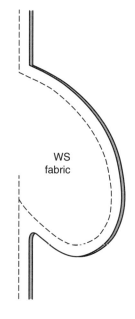

WS
fabric

Hint: Generally it's better to stitch with the grain from the hem to the top, but when stitching the side seamlines, it's more important to stitch both in the same direction.

4. Complete the pocket.

Variation: Yohji Yamamoto Pocket

Design Analysis:

Used on a Yohji Yamamoto cotton skirt, this variation of the All-in-One pocket has French seams on the side seams and around the pocket sacks. On the skirt, the seams are stitched down to look like flat-felled seams.

Sewing Notes:

1. Review the directions for the All-in-One Inseam pocket on page 14.

2. Mark the pocket opening and reinforce as needed.

3. Wrong sides together, match and pin the side seams together. Starting at the top, stitch with a scant 1/4" seam down the side, around the pocket, and down to the hem.

4. Press the seams flat, then to one side. Clip to the stitched line at the bottom of the pocket. Turn the garment wrong side out, and press again, making a fold at the seamline.

5. Complete the French seams on the inside by stitching a generous 1/4" from the edge. Press flat, then press the seams toward the skirt front.

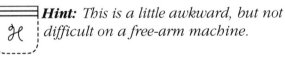 ***Hint:*** *For a slimmer line, always press side seams toward the front to avoid a ridge at the seamline.*

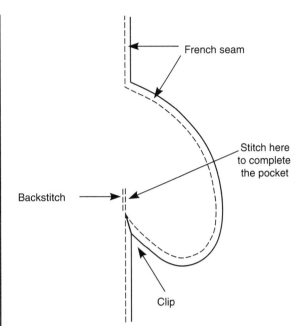

French seam

Stitch here
to complete
the pocket

Backstitch

Clip

6. Complete the pockets by stitching from the bottom of the pocket opening to the seamline below the pocket. Backtack at both ends of the seam.

7. On the skirt front, topstitch the pocket opening 1/4" from the edge, leaving long threads at the beginning and end. Topstitch the side seams 1/4" from the seamline, leaving long threads at the opening. Pull the threads to the underside and tie them securely.

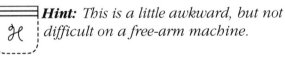 ***Hint:*** *This is a little awkward, but not difficult on a free-arm machine.*

Design Ideas for Inseam Pockets

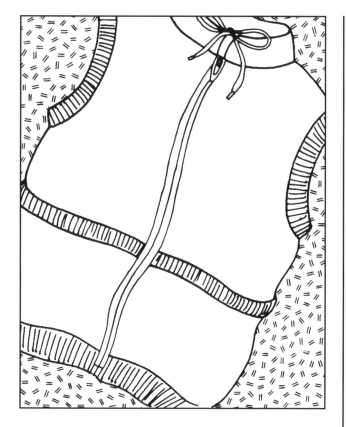

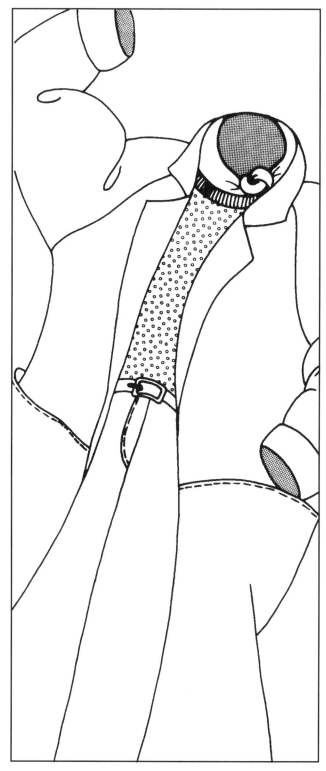

Inseam pockets can be used on almost any material, from knits to leather. Even though they are frequently inconspicuous and utilitarian, they can be used as decorative details and be highlighted with topstitching or accentuated with ribbing.

2. Edge Pockets

Known by a variety of names—structural, stylized, open seam, or decorative inseam pockets—edge pockets are also a type of inseam pocket. They are a conspicuous element of the garment design and are located so that the edge of one garment section against the adjoining section forms the pocket styleline. More diverse than closed-seam pockets, edge pockets range from utilitarian, slanted, side-front pockets to interesting stylized details on dresses, blouses, skirts, jackets, and jeans. If these pockets are replaced by a regular seam, the overall garment design is compromised.

Compared with basic inseam pockets which all look more or less alike, edge pockets vary in shape and detailing. However, a close examination reveals that the construction is similar for both types. Both have an upper pocket which finishes the pocket opening and an underpocket. On edge pockets the underpocket is generally cut in one with the underlay or garment section instead of being cut separately as with inconspicuous inseam pockets.

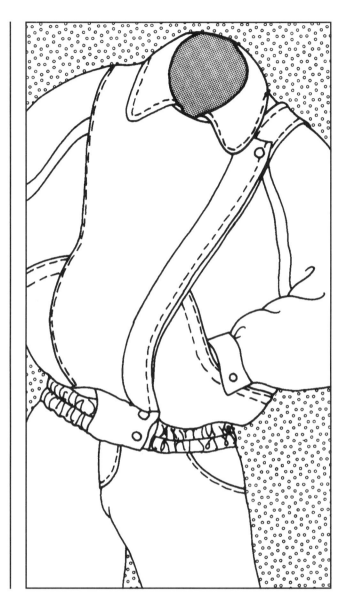

Anatomy of an Edge Pocket

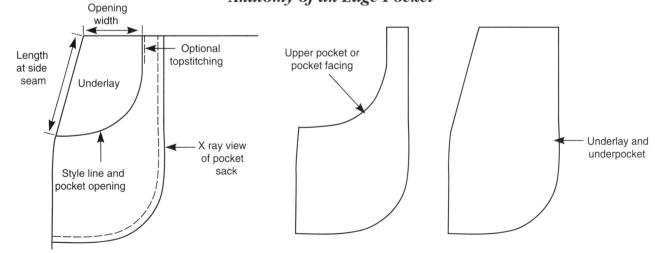

Front-Hip Pockets

There are many different front-hip pockets, such as the slanted front-hip, curved, jeans, and western pockets. Some seasons stylized openings are the fashion. The most popular design is always the slanted side-front pocket, probably because it is the most slenderizing, while jeans and western pockets add visual inches to the hipline.

Front-hip pockets can hug the body or stand away to create a design detail. Generally, the more the pocket stands away from the body, the wider the figure looks and the more the underpocket shows, but stand away pockets can also be used to create exaggerated silhouettes which minimize the waist line.

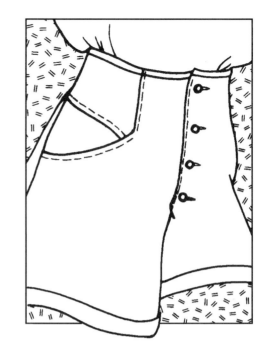

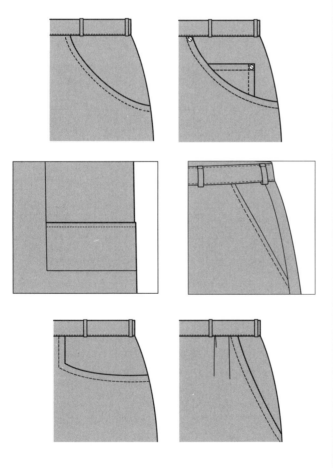

Slanted Front-Hip Pocket

Design Analysis:

The opening for the typical slanted front-hip pocket measures 1-1/8" to 2" wide at the waist and 6-1/2" to 8" long at the side seam. The pocket opening can begin at the waist or it can be topstitched closed for 1" to 1-1/2" below the waist. Some pockets I measured were 1-1/8" by 7-1/2", 1-1/2" by 6-1/2", and 1-1/8" by 7". Generally the more vertical the slant, the more slenderizing the pocket.

For these directions, I measured the pocket on a pair of Yves Saint Laurent trousers. The pocket is 1-1/2" wide at the waist and 8" long. The opening was topstitched closed for 1-1/2" below the waist.

Pattern Development:

1. Review the Pattern Development for the Basic Inseam Pocket on page 4.

2. Draw the pocket opening on the pattern. For tailored trousers, the opening is straight, but it can be shaped on other designs. (See Stylized Edge Pockets.)

To establish the pocket styleline, mark the top of the styleline (A) on the waistline 1-1/2" from the side seam. Mark the bottom of the styleline (B) on the side seam 8" below the waistline seam. Draw styleline AB.

> **Hint:** *If the pocket opening is small and the garment fits closely, the pocket opening will be too tight, the pocket will be difficult to use, and the underpocket will wrinkle unattractively. This problem can be eliminated by adding a little length or ease to the pocket opening so it will lie smoothly over the underpocket. To add the ease, extend line*

AB into the side seam allowance, measure from point B 1/4" to 1/2" and mark point C. On the pattern front, redraw the side seam and its seam allowance so that the seamline connects with point C.

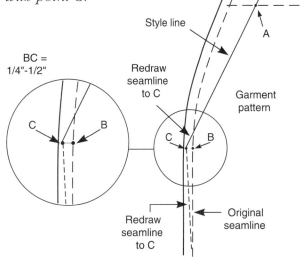

3. On the pattern, pin out any darts or pleats at the waistline.

4. Draw the pocket sack so that the finished pocket will be at least 1" wider than the opening and 2-1/2" deeper. For this design, draw the underpocket 4" wide at the waistline and 11" deep. This establishes the pocket shape and includes the seam allowances at the side and bottom of the pocket sack. Indicate one matchpoint on the pocket styleline and two on the edge of the pocket sack.

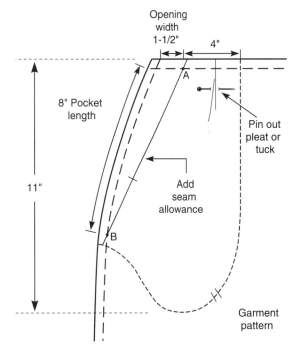

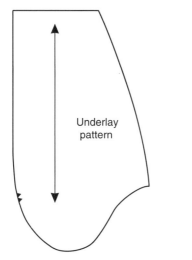
5. To make the pattern for the pocket underlay, on a piece of tracing paper trace the seamlines and cutting lines at the waist and side seam and any matchpoints. Trace the pocket sack, its matchpoints, and the grainline.

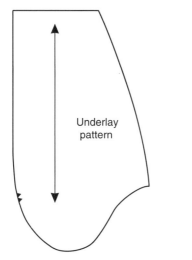

Underlay pattern

Cut two underlay patterns and set one aside for the upper pocket. Since the underlay forms a portion of the garment as well as the underpocket, it is cut from the fashion fabric. If you don't have enough fabric to do this, the underpocket can be cut from lining fabric with a self-fabric facing or it can be cut in two pieces with self-fabric at the top and lining at the bottom. For both, the self-fabric should extend into the pocket enough so that the lining won't show when the garment is worn. Generally, 1-1/4" is enough; however, if the pocket stands away from the body, the underlay will show more and the facing must be longer.

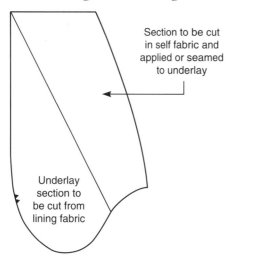

Section to be cut in self fabric and applied or seamed to underlay

Underlay section to be cut from lining fabric

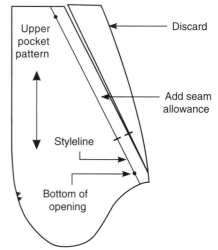
6. Continuing with the darts still pinned out, pin the extra underlay pattern to the garment pattern. Trace the pocket styleline and its matchpoint. Add a seam allowance to the styleline.

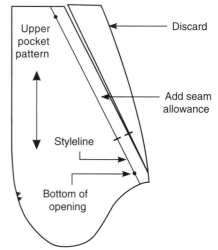

Upper pocket pattern

Discard

Add seam allowance

Styleline

Bottom of opening

On commercial patterns, this is the upper pocket pattern and it is cut from lining material. On better ready-to-wear, it frequently has a self-fabric facing at the top. To make a self-fabric facing at the top, draw the new seamline parallel to the pocket styleline and 1-3/8" below it, and indicate a matchpoint. Cut the pattern apart on the new seamline, and add a seam allowance to each section. On the facing, draw the grainline parallel to the styleline.

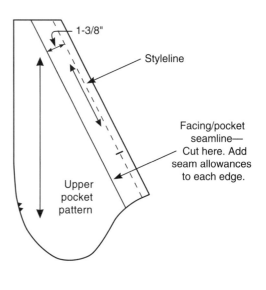

1-3/8"

Styleline

Facing/pocket seamline— Cut here. Add seam allowances to each edge.

Upper pocket pattern

7. To make the new garment-pattern front, unpin the darts or tucks. Trace all unchanged cutting lines, seamlines, and matchpoints. Trace the grainline. Trace the pocket styleline, its matchpoint, and the ends of the opening. Add a seam allowance to the pocket styleline.

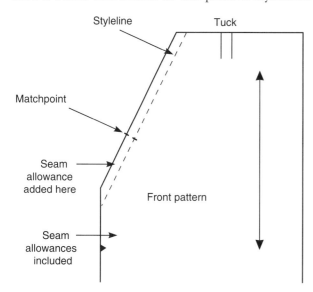

Sewing Notes:

1. Review the Sewing Notes for the Basic Inseam Pocket on page 6.

2. Cut the underlay from self-fabric and the upper pocket from the lining.

3. Mark the pocket opening, and reinforce as needed (see page 6).

4. Right sides together, match and pin the garment front and upper pocket at the pocket styleline. Stitch and press. If you don't plan to topstitch the edge, understitch. Trim, clip, and grade the seam. Press.

Hint: Although you can stitch the entire edge, I prefer to end my stitching when I reach the side seam at the bottom of the opening. Then I clip to the end of the stitched line. With this method, there is less bulk in the side seam because when the pocket

is turned to the inside, the unstitched seam allowance remains flat. You should experiment with both methods to see which you like better.

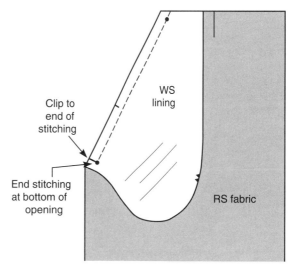

5. Turn the pocket to the inside and press the edge.

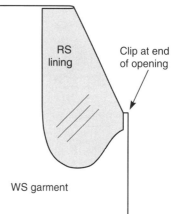

6. On tailored trousers, topstitch the opening 1/4" from the edge. On dressier designs, edgestitch the opening or leave the edge plain and just understitch.

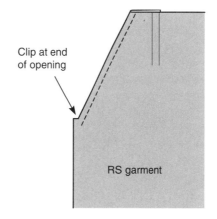

7. Right side up, lay the underlay on the table. Cover it with the front, right side up. Match and pin the edges together at the waist and side seam. Turn the sections over and pin the pocket sacks together. Stitch around the edges of the pocket and finish the raw edges. Press.

8. Right sides together, join the garment front and back. Stitch the side seams, and press. Baste the top of the pocket to the garment waistline.

Hint: *Clip the side seam as needed so the seam allowances can be pressed open below the pocket.*

9. Pin the pocket styleline flat against the underlay and stitch from the waistline to the beginning of the pocket opening or about 1-1/2".

Stitch the edge flat against the underlay

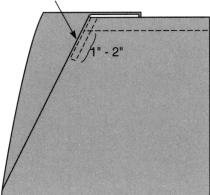

1" - 2"

Hint: *For most designs, I prefer machine stitching at the edge. On sports wear, I stitch again 1/4" away. On dressy pants, I sometimes use a hand fell stitch.*

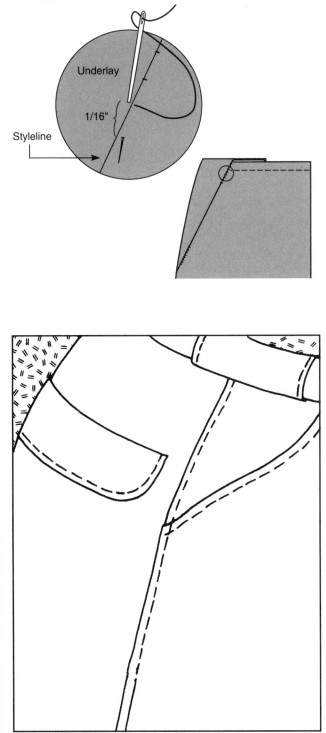

Underlay

1/16"

Styleline

Stand-Away Pocket

A variation of the basic Slanted Front-Hip Pocket, the Stand-Away Pocket is cut so that the pocket styleline is longer than the underlay. It can be used on skirts, pants, blouses, and dresses.

Used by Adrienne Vittadini on a princess-line dress in a recent collection, this stand-away pocket is located at the bottom of the side-front panel.

The size of the pocket, underpocket depth, and amount it stands away vary with the design of the garment and the location of the pocket. The more the pocket stands away, the more the underpocket will show. Generally, the pocket depth should measure at least 6" from the opening unless the depth is limited by the length of the garment or garment section.

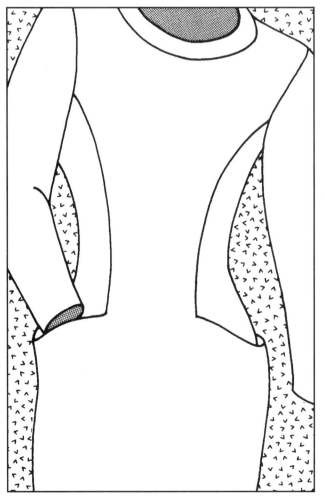

Pattern Development:

1. Begin with a commercial pattern that already has appropriate seamlines for your design, then review Pattern Development for the Slanted Front-Hip Pocket on page 23.

2. Indicate the pocket opening on the front and side-front garment patterns, and mark a match point.

3. On the garment front pattern, use a colored pencil or dashes to draw the pocket sack 6" deep. Add 5/8" seam allowances. Mark two matchpoints on the edge of the pocket sack.

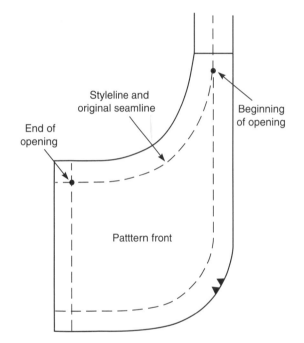

Styleline and original seamline

End of opening

Beginning of opening

Patttern front

Hint: If the pocket is near a vertical seamline, make the pocket sack wide enough so the side of the pocket can be sewn into the side seam.

4. To make the pocket sack patterns, trace the seamlines, cutting lines, matchpoints, and grainline from the front pattern onto a piece of pattern paper. Make two copies, one for the upper pocket and one for the underpocket.

5. To make the new side-front pattern with an attached underlay, pin one of the pocket sacks you made in Step 4 to the original side-front pattern, matching the seamlines. Trace the new pattern.

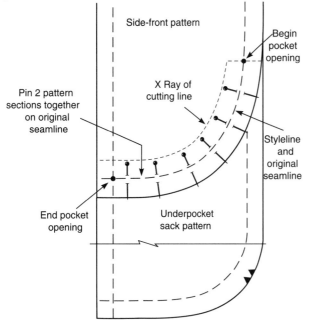

Pin 2 pattern sections together on original seamline

Side-front pattern

Begin pocket opening

X Ray of cutting line

Styleline and original seamline

End pocket opening

Underpocket sack pattern

6. To establish the pocket styleline on the garment front pattern so the pocket will stand away, draw a 6" line perpendicular to the styleline. Cut the line, and place a piece of paper under the slash. Spread the edge 1" and tape it open. Redraw the styleline and side seam as needed so they will be smooth without odd angles.

Then, to make a new garment front pattern, trace the seamlines, cutting lines, matchpoints, and grainline on a piece of pattern paper.

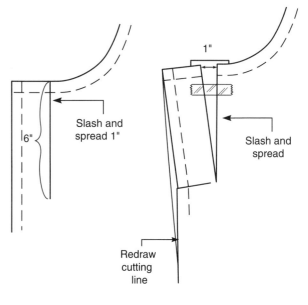

1"

Slash and spread 1"

6"

Slash and spread

Redraw cutting line

 Hints: *To make the pocket stand away more, make the slash longer and spread the edges more.*

On some designs, you may prefer to enlarge the entire front section instead of just the styleline. You can do this by slashing to the hemline and spreading the entire section the desired amount. Or you can use the pivot and slide method.

7. Slash and spread the upper pocket pattern as you did the garment pattern in step 6 so that the edges which will be joined together are the same length.

If the garment section was slashed to the hemline, slash the upper pocket pattern only to the seamline at the bottom of the sack to avoid making the seamline on the upper pocket longer than that on the underpocket.

Sewing Notes:

1. Review the Sewing Notes for the Basic Side Pocket on page 6.

2. To prevent the pocket from collapsing, interface the styleline on the front sections. The exact size and shape of the interfacing will depend on the fashion fabric as well as on the amount the pocket stands away.

Hints: I begin with a rectangle of sew-in interfacing about 2" wider than the pocket styleline and 6" long. I pin it to the pocket styleline on the wrong side of the front. After the garment is assembled, I examine the interfacing's effect. If it's too long or wide, I trim trim as needed.

If the section is backed or underlined, the styleline may not need a separate interfacing.

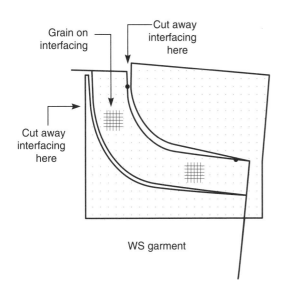

Grain on interfacing

Cut away interfacing here

Cut away interfacing here

WS garment

3. Since the pocket stands away, the upper pocket will show when the garment is worn. Cut the upper pocket from self-fabric or cut it in two pieces with a self-fabric facing at the styleline and a lining pocket sack.

Stylized Pockets

The basic Front-Hip Pocket can easily be modified to create a variety of stylized pockets by reshaping the styleline, inserting pipings, adding cuffs, folding the edge back, or just binding the edge. On some designs, minor changes are made on the pattern; on others, changes can be made when you sew.

Novelty Stylelines:

The pocket opening can be reshaped almost any way you want. Here are some novelty stylelines to consider: curved, scalloped, western, and frog's mouth.

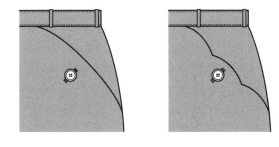

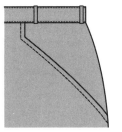
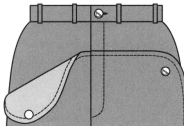

An attractive formula for most curved skirt pockets is to make the length twice the width, i.e., 2-3/4" wide by 5-1/2" long. But on jeans, the curved pocket is usually wide and short. Some good proportions are: 3-3/4" wide by 2" long and 3-3/4" wide by 3" long. For a western pocket, 6" wide by 1-3/8" long is a nice design.

Hint: When considering a different or unusual styleline, experiment with paper patterns in several proportions and "try them on" on your dress form or yourself to determine which is most attractive. On skirts, I cut a paper pattern just for the visible portion of a new pocket, and pin it onto the skirt I'm wearing. Then, standing at least 6' from the mirror, I examine the design.

Make the pattern with a separate upper pocket and assemble the design using the method of your choice.

Styleline Trims:

To define the pocket styleline with pizzazz, use a piping or binding. Since the two are similar when finished, choose the one which is more compatible with the construction techniques on the rest of the garment and your sewing ability.

Pipings and Bindings:

To add a piping, baste the piping to the pocket styleline at the outset, before the upper pocket is sewn. Then complete the pocket in the usual manner.

To add a binding, trim away the seam allowances of both the garment and upper pocket at the styleline. Wrong sides together, baste the sections together, then bind the edge using the material and method of your choice.

Changing Edge Pockets to Basic Inseam Pockets:

Many skirt and trouser patterns have slanted front-hip pockets—the most popular, Edge or Open Seam Pocket. This design is more difficult to fit than garments with the Basic Inseam Pocket. It's also not as dressy and requires more fabric to sew. Use these directions to change a pattern with edge pockets to a Basic Inseam Pocket.

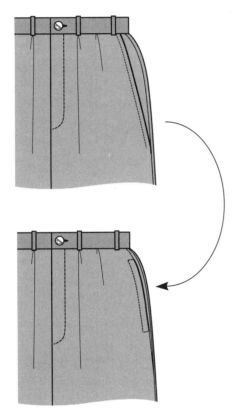

1. Identify and discard the upper pocket pattern or pocket sack which joins the garment front. On some patterns it's called the pocket facing or inside pocket.

2. Identify the underlay, which joins the garment back but is visible as a part of the front. On some patterns this section is called the front inset or underpocket.

3. Pin the underlay to the garment front so the matchpoints are aligned.

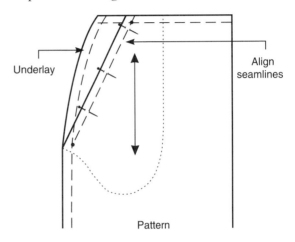

4. Make a new front pattern by tracing the outer edges of the front and underlay, indicating all matchpoints and notches on the edges.

Indicate the new pocket opening on the traced pattern. It should be about 6" long and begin 1" to 2" below the waistline seam. (See Pattern Development for the Basic Inseam Pocket on page 4.)

5. For each pocket, rename the original underlay "pocket sack" and label it "cut two"—for one underpocket and one upper pocket.

Design Ideas for Edge Pockets

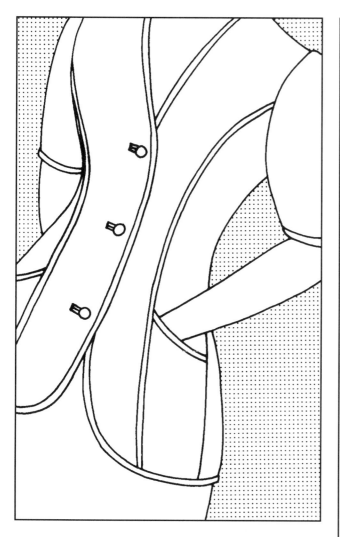

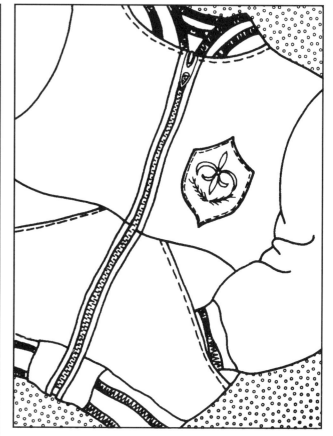

Perfect for a variety of designs from casual to dressy, edge pockets form an integral element of the design. They can range from simple straight openings to interesting novelty designs.

3. More Inseam Pockets

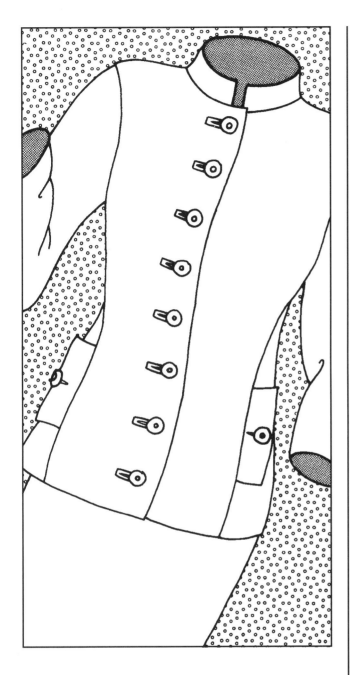

In addition to the basic inseam pockets and edge pockets already described, there are many more inseam pockets ranging from practical, easy-sew pockets with plackets to stylized pockets that are more decorative than useful and pockets with figure-flattering tummy control panels.

Most of the pockets described in this section can be modified easily to develop many different pockets, and most are suitable for both types of inseam pockets: closed and edge.

Inseam Pocket With a Welt

Design Analysis:

At first glance the Inseam Pocket With a Welt looks like the more difficult and time-consuming Applied Welt Pocket. By contrast, it is easier to sew and can be used on seams or darts. These directions for an inseam pocket can be adapted for edge pockets.

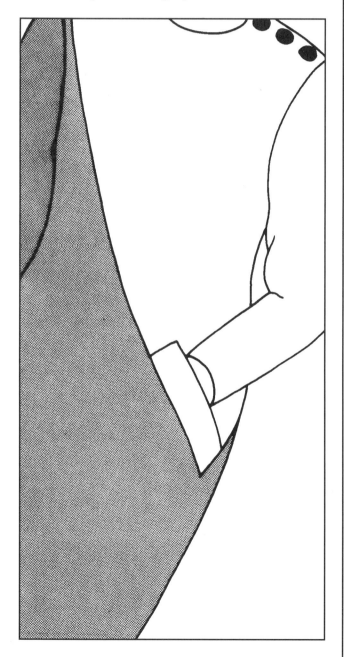

Pattern Development:

1. To make the pattern for the upper pocket, review Pattern Development for the Basic Inseam Pocket on page 4.

2. To make the pattern for the underpocket, review Pattern Development for the All-in-One Inseam Pocket on page 14.

> **Hint:** *If you don't have enough fabric to use an all-in-one pocket for the underpocket, use a self-fabric under-pocket, self-fabric facing, or an extension on the garment.*

3. Make a welt pattern. (See Welts and Flaps on page 106.)

Sewing Notes:

1. Review the Sewing Notes for the Basic Inseam Pocket on page X and for Welts and Flaps on page X.

2. Mark the pocket opening on each garment section, and reinforce appropriately for the garment quality.

3. Complete the welt. Topstitch and add a buttonhole if desired.

4. With the garment front (or lower section) right side up, position and pin the welt face-down on the garment front. Machine baste just inside the seamline.

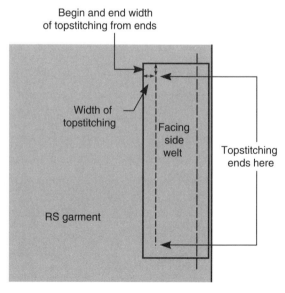

Begin and end width of topstitching from ends

Width of topstitching

Facing side welt

Topstitching ends here

RS garment

5. Continuing with the garment right side up, position and pin the upper pocket face-down on the welt/garment section. Stitch on the seamline. Begin and end at the ends of the opening. Understitch, grade, and press.

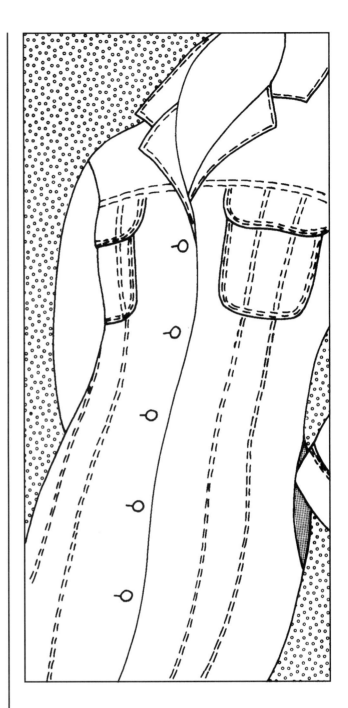

Hint: *When grading the pocket seam, the garment seam allowance which is nearest the outside of the garment is always the longest, and the upper pocket seam allowance, shortest.*

6. With right sides together, join the garment front (or lower section) and back (or upper section). Stop and start at the ends of the opening. Press.

7. Complete the pocket by joining the pocket sacks. Begin and end at the ends of the opening. Clip the seam allowance as needed so it will lie flat when pressed open.

8. Secure the ends of the welt.

Inseam Pocket With a Flap

Design Analysis:

Like the Inseam Pocket with a Welt, the Inseam Pocket with a Flap is frequently used on outer wear. It can be used on inseam edge pockets and can have the flap sewn to either edge of the opening. When the flap is sewn to the back or top of the opening, it conceals the opening itself and frequently has a button. By contrast, when the flap is sewn to the front or bottom, it leaves the opening exposed and is sometimes called a cuff.

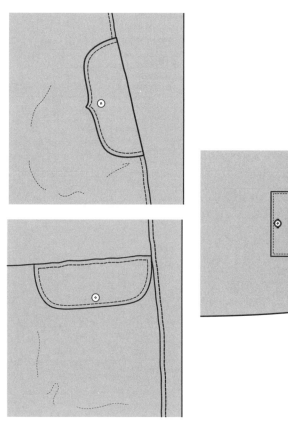

When adapting these directions for an edge pocket, you must add a seam on the pocket underlay, at the styleline, for inserting the flap. When this is done, it then becomes an inseam pocket.

Pattern Development:

1. Review the Pattern Development for the Basic Inseam Pocket (see page 4) and make the pocket pattern.

2. Review the Pattern Development for Welts and Flaps and make a flap pattern (see page 108.)

Sewing Notes:

1. Mark the pocket opening and reinforce appropriately.

2. Cut a self-fabric underpocket and a lining upper pocket.

3. Complete the flap. See Welts and Flaps on page 106.)

4. To sew the flap to the front (or bottom) of the opening, begin with the garment and flap right side up. Baste the flap to the garment front so the ends of the flap are at the ends of the opening.

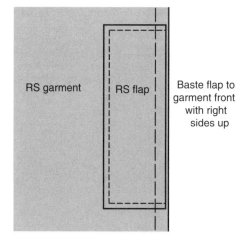

RS garment   RS flap   Baste flap to garment front with right sides up

5. Right sides together, join the upper pocket and garment section on the seamline. You are sewing through garment, flap, and upper pocket. Begin and end precisely at the ends of the opening. (This should also be the ends of the flap.) Clip to the ends of the opening. Understitch, trim, and press.

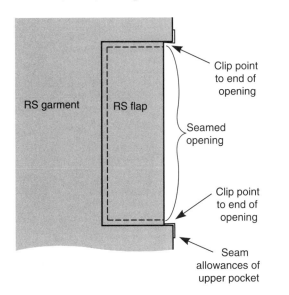

Hint: To clip precisely to the ends of the opening, use scissors which cut to the ends of the points. Position the scissors exactly where the clip should be and close them.

6. With the garment/upper pocket side of the pocket up, position the underpocket face down on the pocket, right sides together. Pin the underpocket to the upper pocket. Stitch around the pocket bag.

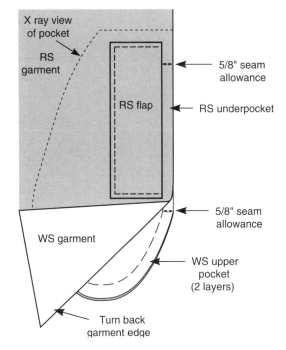

7. If the pocket has a flap at the back (or top) of the opening instead of at the front, baste it, right side up, to the seam allowance at the top of the underpocket.

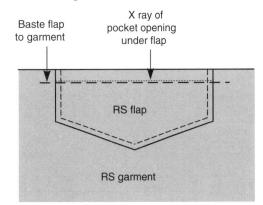

In this case, when the flap covers the opening, make the opening 1/2" shorter than the flap (1/4" on each side).

8. Right sides together, join the garment sections on the seamline.

Edge Pockets With Cuffs

There are two types of cuffs for edge pockets: separate and turn-back. Separate cuffs are inserted into the seamline like a flap while turn-back cuffs are created by facing the pocket edge attractively and folding it back to make the cuff.

To add a separate cuff, design and assemble the cuff (see Appendix, Welts and Flaps), then sew it into the pocket styleline. (See Sewing Notes for Inseam Pocket with a Flap.)

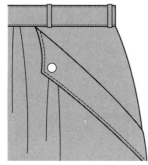

Turn-back cuffs can be any shape. For your first design, begin with a frog's mouth or curved pocket and a self-fabric upper pocket. (See *Sew Any Patch Pocket*, page 43.)

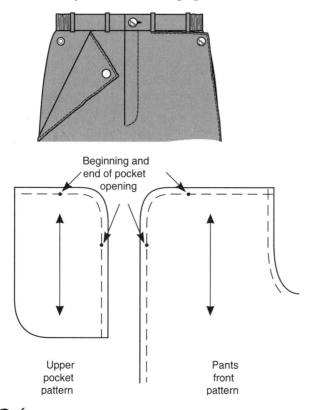

Beginning and end of pocket opening

Upper pocket pattern

Pants front pattern

Hint: I cut the upper pocket pattern 1/8" to 1/4" wider and 1/4" to 3/8" longer than usual to allow for the turn of the cloth so the cuff will turn back smoothly. The amount of extra depends on the fabric—the thicker the fabric, the more fabric is needed, so the amount varies. I also interface most cuffs with a lightweight fusible to support the cuff shape.

Sewing Notes:

1. Review the Sewing Notes for the Basic Inseam Pocket on page 6.

2. To make the cuff, baste the upper pocket to the pocket opening.

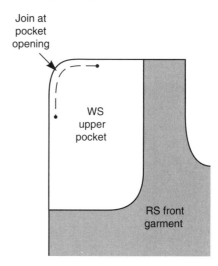

Join at pocket opening

WS upper pocket

RS front garment

3. Right sides together, sew around the edges of the cuff, beginning and ending at the ends of the opening.

4. Clip to the ends of the opening, trim, and grade the seam allowances. Press.

5. Turn the cuff right side out with the upper pocket on the inside of the garment. Press.

6. Right sides together, join the underpocket to the upper pocket.

Outline Pocket

Design Analysis:

On the Outline Pocket, the pocket sack is topstitched against the body of the garment. It is particularly attractive on casual designs and fabrics such as velour, terry, and bulky knits. On reversible garments, the pocket sack forms a patch pocket on the reverse side. It can be made as usual with two pocket sacks, or it can be made with just an underpocket, using the garment itself as the upper pocket. For the latter, the pocket opening can be finished with a narrow topstitched hem or a flat blindstitched or fused hem.

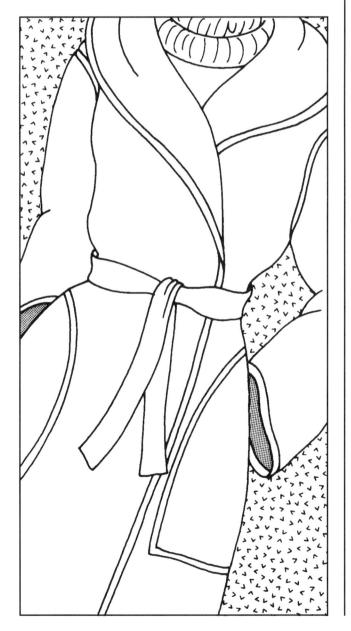

These directions are for an inseam pocket with one pocket sack—the underpocket which many seamsters prefer—because it has less bulk. The technique can be adapted for two-sack pockets, edge pockets, and even slash pockets.

Pattern Development:

To make the underpocket, review the Pattern Development for the Basic Inseam Pocket on page 4 and make a pattern with an Extension.

Hint: *If you have plenty of fabric, use the All-in-One Inseam Pocket for the underpocket.*

Sewing Notes:

1. Review the Sewing Notes for the Basic Inseam Pocket on page 6 and the Inseam Pocket with an Extension on page 12.

2. Cut the underpocket from self-fabric or lining fabric. There is no upper pocket.

3. Mark the pocket opening, and reinforce as needed.

4. On the front (or lower edge) of the pocket opening, finish the raw edge of the extension with serging, zigzagging, pinking, or seam tape.

5. Right sides together, join the underpocket and garment back (or top) at the opening with a 1/4" parallel seam. Press.

6. Right sides together, pin the garment front and back together. Stitch the seam. Stop and start at the ends of the pocket opening and backstitch.

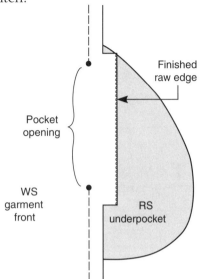

Finished raw edge

Pocket opening

WS garment front

RS underpocket

7. Press the seam open, then press the extension and underpocket toward the front (or down). Clip the seam allowance to the seamline at the ends of the opening so the seam will lie flat when pressed open.

8. Hem the opening on the garment front invisibly with a blindstitch or catchstitch or, for casual garments, topstitch the opening.

> *Hint:* You can fuse the extension to the wrong side of the garment if it won't show on the right side of the garment. Always test first.

9. Finish the raw edges of the seam and pocket sack.

> *Hint:* On reversible garments, bind the edges of the pocket with bias binding or finish with decorative serging.

10. Wrong side up, carefully smooth and pin the underpocket to the wrong side of the garment front.

> *Hint:* Set the pins near the edges of the pocket sack so you can use them as a guide.

11. Right side up, use a temporary marking pen, chalk, soap sliver, or thread tracing to mark the stitching line for the pocket. Baste the pocket in place if needed.

> *Hint:* When marking a pair of pockets, use a freezer paper template so the pockets will be identical.

12. Right side up, topstitch around the pocket. Pull any thread ends to the underside and knot. Press.

> *Hint:* When using this pocket on sports wear or casual designs, topstitch the seams as well as the pocket.

Variation: Outline Pocket With Two Sacks

Generally, I prefer the Outline Pocket with Two Sacks because the inside of the pocket is a little smoother. Also, the pocket sacks can be joined with a French seam for a clean finish on the inside of the garment and on reversible garments (see the Yohji Yamamoto Variation on page 15), or you can quilt the upper pocket to the garment.

Sewing Notes:

1. Complete the Inseam or Edge Pocket using your favorite method.

2. Finish the seam and pocket edges.

> *Hint:* On reversible garments, join the pocket sacks with a French seam, bind the edges with bias binding, or finish them with decorative serging.

3. Right side up, pin and topstitch the pocket in place.

Side Pocket With Control Panel

Design Analysis:

Suitable for all inseam pockets, this pocket has a panel that extends from one pocket across the front to the other pocket. In addition to preserving the garment's shape so the pleats or gathers hang properly and the pockets don't gap, the panel also serves as a tummy control. Generally, the garment will hang more attractively when it has a zipper at the center back rather than a fly zipper. These directions can be adapted for Edge Pockets.

Pattern Development:

Cut the control panel and upper pocket in one piece to avoid bulk, and cut the underpocket separately.

1. Review the Pattern Development for the Basic Inseam Pocket on page 4 and make a pattern.

2. To make the pattern for the control panel, pin the upper pocket pattern to a new piece of pattern paper. Pin out any darts, pleats, or gathers on the front pattern. Then match and pin the pocket opening to the pattern front.

Trace the center front and waistline seamlines. Begin 7" below the waist at the center front then curve down to the lower edge of the pocket, creating a smooth curve. Add seam allowances as needed, and indicate the grainline.

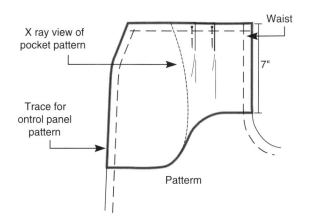

X ray view of pocket pattern

Trace for control panel pattern

Patterm

Waist

7"

Hint: *If the garment doesn't have a seam at the center front, I cut the control panel without a seam. But when working with an untried pattern, I prefer to add a center-front seam with 1" seam allowances so that I can adjust the panel width, if necessary. Also, it's easier to stitch the underpocket to the control panel when the panel has a center-front seam.*

Sewing Notes:

1. Review the Sewing Notes for the Basic Inseam Pocket on page 6.

2. Cut the control panel from a lightweight, firmly woven fabric, stretch lace, power net, or two-way stretch fabric. Cut the underpocket from self-fabric. If the control panel color will show at the pocket opening, cut and apply a facing to the control panel.

3. Mark the pocket opening and reinforce it appropriately.

4. Right sides together, join the control panel and front at the pocket opening. Clip the seam allowances to the ends of the pocket opening. Press, understitch, and turn right sides out.

5. Pocket side up, lay the front/panel section flat. Cover it with the underpocket so that the right sides of the two pocket sections are together. Match and pin the underpocket and control panel together. Stitch around the underpocket with a straight stitch, holding the front out of the way. Then stitch again over the raw edges with a zigzag stitch (W,2-L,2).

6. If the control panel has a center-front seam, pin it and check the fit. Stitch it separately.

Hint: *Generally it's better to stitch this seam so the seam allowances are between the garment and the control panel, but it can be stitched with the seam toward the body.*

7. When the garment has a zipper at center front, pin the control panel out of the way so you can set the zipper easily. To finish the control panel, turn under the raw edges and hand sew them to the back of the zipper.

8. Baste the top of the control panel to the waistline and complete the garment.

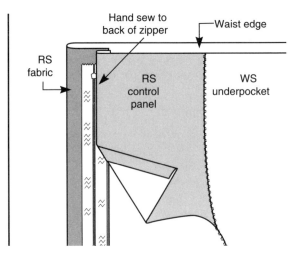

Variation: Clotilde's Proper Pocket

To keep your pockets from popping out when you sit, Clotilde designed the Proper Pocket for her book *Sew Smart Supplement.* It has a rectangular stay to control the pockets. It is not only quick and easy to make, but can also be added to ready-made designs.

1. To add the stay to a finished garment, estimate the width between the two pockets and add 2" for seams. Cut the stay pattern this width and 8" deep.

2. Cut the stay from a firm lining fabric with a selvage at one long edge.

3. With the selvage toward the hem baste the stay to the pocket sacks. Adjust the width as needed for your figure, then stitch permanently.

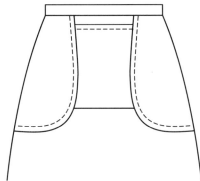

Easy Pocket Placket

Design Analysis:

A substitute for a zipper placket, the placket in a pocket is the perfect answer if zippers are your nemesis. This easy technique is used by American designers like Calvin Klein and Oscar de la Renta and doesn't require a zipper. It can be used for skirts and pants with one pocket, but the design is generally more attractive with a pair of pockets. On the left side, the pocket opening begins at the waistline. On the right side, it begins 1-1/4" to 2" below the waist.

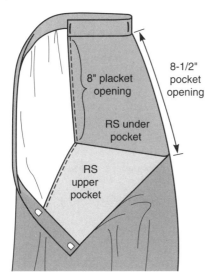

The left pocket sack is left unstitched for at least 8-1/2" to form the placket opening. The waistband has an underlap extension at the top of the pocket sack.

These directions can be adapted for the Side Pocket with an Extension and for Edge Pockets.

Pattern Development:

1. Review the Pattern Development for a Basic Inseam Pocket on page 4.

On the side seams of the skirt pattern, mark the bottom of the pocket opening 8-1/2" below the waistline. On the right side, mark the top of the pocket 1-1/2" to 2" below the waistline.

2. Draw the pocket sack pattern 5" wide and 13" long, including seam allowances. Indicate the grainline.

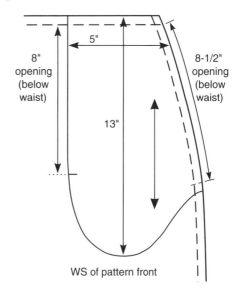

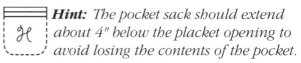 **Hint:** *The pocket sack should extend about 4" below the placket opening to avoid losing the contents of the pocket.*

3. Mark the placket opening on the pocket sack, 8" below the waistline.

Hint: *If you have large hips and plan to step into the garment, you may need a longer opening or a placket on both sides. To determine the length you need, subtract your waist measurement from your hip measurement, then divide by two. For a 32" waist and 50" hips, make the opening 9" long or make two plackets. (50" minus 32" = 18" divided by 2 = 9".)*

4. Extend the underlap on the waistband pattern as needed (here, about 5") so there will be enough band to sew to the top of the underpocket. The extension must be as long as the underpocket at the waistline plus a seam allowance.

Sewing Notes:

1. Review the Sewing Notes for the Basic Inseam Pocket on page 6.

2. Mark the pocket and placket openings.

3. Reinforce the pocket opening as needed to prevent stretching.

4. Cut the underpocket from self-fabric and cut the upperpocket from lining.

5. On the pocket sacks for the left side pocket, finish the placket opening with a narrow machine-stitched hem or by serging.

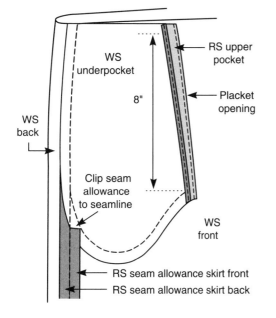

6. Right sides together, join the upper pocket and skirt front at the side seam. Press, understitch, and turn to the wrong side.

7. Right side up, lay the underlay on the table. Cover it with the front right side up. Match and pin the edges together at the waist and side seam. Turn the section over and pin the pocket sacks together.

8. Join the pocket sacks and finish the raw edges of the pocket.

Hint: Oscar de la Renta joins the sacks with a French seam. First join the sack wrong sides together. Clip the corner at the side seam extension, turn the sack right sides together, stitch again, and press.

9. Topstitch the pocket opening if desired.

10. Right sides together, join the front to the back at the side seam. Press. Topstitch the seam, if desired.

11. Adjust any gathers, pleats, etc., on the skirt.

12. Pin the upper pocket to the wrong side of the skirt front at the waist and baste them together on the waist seamline.

13. Using your favorite method, prepare and set the waistband.

Variation: Zipper Placket Pocket

Design Analysis:

The Zipper Placket Pocket can be completed in less than five minutes. It begins with a Basic Inseam Pocket and a self-fabric underpocket. The underpocket is cut into two sections and the zipper is set with the teeth exposed.

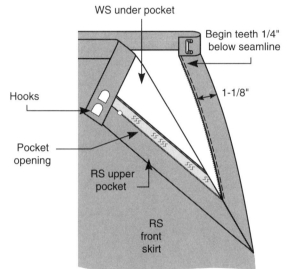

Sewing Notes:

1. Review the directions for the Basic Inseam Pocket on page 4.

2. Cut the underpocket from self-fabric and the upper pocket from lining.

3. On the underpocket, draw the zipper opening about 2" from the side seam edge with a temporary marking pen or chalk. Cut on the marked line.

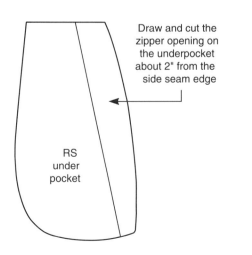

Draw and cut the zipper opening on the underpocket about 2" from the side seam edge

4. Right sides together, with the zipper teeth 7/8" below the top edge, stitch one edge of the underpocket to the zipper tape with a 1/4" seam. Repeat for the other edge.

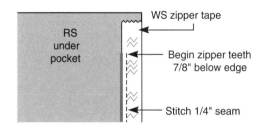

5. Press lightly so the zipper is exposed, then, right side up, edgestitch next to the zipper seamline if desired.

6. Below the zipper, press the 1/4" seam allowances to the wrong side. Butt and zigzag the folded edges together.

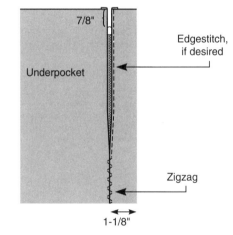

7. Complete the pocket.

Design Ideas for More Inseam Pockets

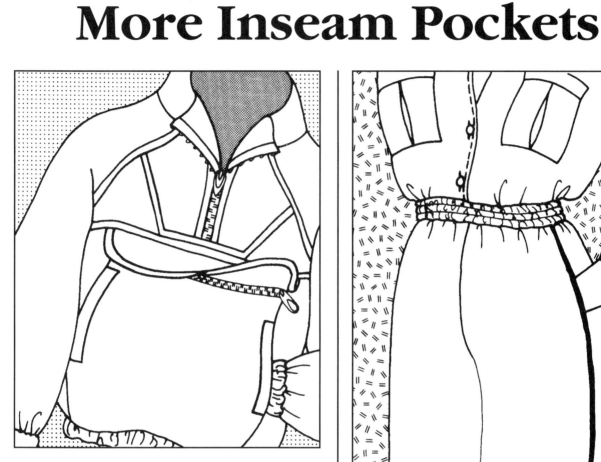

The diversity of inseam pockets is never-ending. They can be finished with a zipper at the opening or hidden under decorative bound seams.

Part II:

Slash Pockets

Frequently used on expensive ready-to-wear, slash pockets run the gamut from the simple porthole pocket to the elegant applied welt. They are often reserved for dressy garments, fabrics which will be dry-cleaned, and designs for adults, but they can be used on all types of garments and any fabric.

Welts are used on all types of tailored garments: jackets, coats, vests, shirts, skirts, trousers, and dresses. Straight or shaped, they can be decorative or utilitarian. They can be located on any grain—vertically, horizontally, or on a slant, and are particularly attractive on plain, closely woven fabrics.

Slash pockets can be used alone or with a flap or button tab. When made without a flap, they are generally more decorative than utilitarian because they are not as strong and tend to gap when used.

Before making slash pockets on the garment section, consider the fabric weight, fabric texture and design, as well as the garment design, your sewing skills, time available, and personal preference—then experiment with several methods. The size and depth of the pocket is determined by the type of garment, size and sex of the wearer, and the pocket's location.

Pockets can be placed horizontally, vertically, or on a slant. In fact, many horizontal pockets are actually slanted so the end nearer the garment center is 1/8" higher. When used for a single breast pocket, the slant is 3/4" to 1" with the end toward the armscye higher. When used at the hipline, the slant can be 2" to 3", and even though they generally slant upward toward the garment center, they can also slant downward.

Generally, the pocket opening, the only part that shows on the finished garment, ranges from 3-1/2" to 8" wide and 3/8" to 1/2" deep, while the pocket depth—the unseen portion of the pocket—varies from 3" to 8".

Similar pockets vary in size, but generally they are smaller on ladies' and children's garments and smaller above the waist. For example, on ladies' jackets below the waist, pockets are 5" to 6" wide while the breast pocket is only 3-1/2" to 4" wide. On men's jackets, the lower pockets measure 6" to 6-1/2" and the breast pocket 4-1/8" to 4-1/2".

The pocket depths reflect similar differences: 3" to 4" on bodices, 5" or 6" on skirts and ladies' jackets, and 7" to 8" on men's jackets.

On couture and expensive ready-to-wear, plaids and stripes are usually cut to match the garment section. When darts or seamlines make it impossible to match the fabric pattern to the entire section, the end nearer the center front is matched. For a wide single welt, the welt is matched to the bottom of the opening, while flaps are matched at the top of the opening.

When compared to patch pockets and inseam pockets, slash pockets are much less forgiving because once cut they can rarely be moved or improved. Actually, they aren't that difficult. *You can expect professional results if you work with precision at every step—marking, stitching, cutting, and pressing.*

Standards for Slash Pockets

1. Most slash pockets should be considered decorative, not utilitarian.

2. When worn, the garment should fit the body smoothly and without any visible signs of the pocket sack or seams underneath.

3. Functional pockets should be located so they're convenient to use, and openings should be large enough so that the hand can be inserted easily. However, a few pockets such as watch pockets are always small.

4. The garment should be interfaced under the pocket opening so that it doesn't sag when the pocket is used normally. The interfacing should not show on the right side of the garment.

5. Pocket openings should be "on grain" and rectangular except when designed otherwise for special effects.

6. Pocket openings should be smooth and firm. They should be finished at the corners so thread ends are securely fastened and don't show. Corners should not ravel, pull out, or pucker.

7. Pockets which will be used extensively should be reinforced at the ends of the opening so they won't tear.

8. The opening should not gap and the underpocket should not show. On all better garments the underpockets are made of self-fabric or have a self-fabric facing under the opening.

9. The grain on the pocket facing or underpocket should duplicate the grain of the garment section.

10. Welts should be straight, even in width, flat, and firm enough to hold their shape when the pocket is used. They should be cut precisely on the appropriate grain.

11. Flaps and applied welts duplicate the grain of the garment except when designed otherwise. When this is not possible on designs made of patterned fabrics, the edge nearer the garment center matches the garment.

12. Any topstitching should appear continuous without bald spots or overlapping.

13. The pocket sack should be made of a durable fabric and have the same care requirements as the garment fabric. It should be sturdy enough to withstand the expected use and wear without being too heavy for the garment fabric.

14. Pocket sacks should be bulk-free and invisible or at least inconspicuous from the right side of the garment. They should be smooth so that they don't curl or pull at the edges. The edges should be finished appropriately.

15. On pockets located beneath or adjacent to seamlines, the pocket sack should be shaped so that it will be sewn into the seamline for added strength.

16. The depth of the pocket should be appropriate for the pocket location and use. It should not be so deep that the pocket sack extends into the hem area or beyond the edge of the garment.

17. Paired pockets should be identical in size, shape, location, and grain.

18. Applied welts and flaps used with slash pockets should meet the standards described in Welts and Flaps.

Sidebar

The Semantics of the Welt Pocket

The semantics of the welt pocket are more than a little confusing. The width and depth of the pocket opening are determined by the width and length of each welt, while the finished width of the opening is the same as the finished length of the welts. The finished depth of the opening is the finished widths of the two welts added together.

Fortunately, our illustrator Pam Poole can make anything, even welt pockets, look simple.

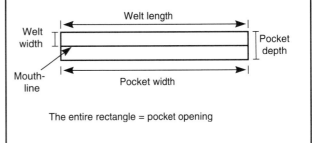

The entire rectangle = pocket opening

4. Basic Slash Pocket

Before making slash pockets on the garment section, always make a sample in a scrap of the fashion fabric. This allows you not only to practice your sewing skills but also to experiment with different methods and to fine-tune the size of the welts.

Design Analysis:

Located in a slash on the body of the garment, slash pockets are designed so that only the opening is visible on the outside of the garment. The pocket sack is hidden inside. Generally identified by the opening itself, there are many different kinds of slash pockets, from simple faced openings to complicated applied welts, and an even greater number of ways to create them. But the pattern and construction of the pocket sack remain more or less unchanged.

These general directions for developing the pocket sack patterns and sewing the pocket apply to most slash pockets, from simple portholes to complex welts. Special techniques for specific designs and variations are found later in the book.

Pattern Development for Pocket Opening:

1. Outline the pocket opening on the paper pattern.

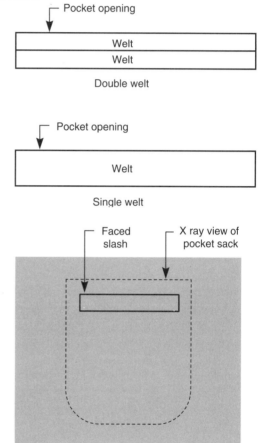

Hint: *If the pocket will cross a seam, pin the pattern sections together on the seamlines at the outset. If it will cross a dart, pin the dart closed.*

If the pocket is utilitarian or the design traditional, locate the pocket so it will be convenient to use and design it with an opening that is large enough for the hand to be inserted easily.

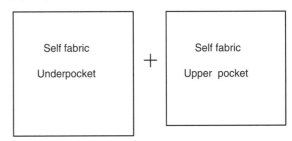

Hint: *If you're using a pattern with patch pockets, locate the opening at the top or one side of the patch pocket.*

If the pocket is purely decorative, it can be any size and located anywhere.

2. Review the pattern development for the pocket you're designing.

Pattern Development for Pocket Sacks:

Every slash pocket has a pocket sack composed of the *underpocket*, which is next to the body or lining, and the *upper pocket*, which is between the underpocket and the outer garment. That seems straightforward, but when sewn, the underpocket is sewn to the top of the pocket opening and the upper pocket to the bottom.

The pocket sack can be cut in an all-in-one section (see drawing on page 57) or in two sections. The pattern companies generally favor the all-in-one, but since it is more difficult to stitch precisely, it is one reason homesewers have so much difficulty with slash pockets.

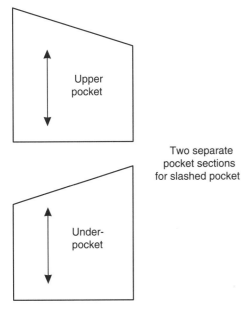

Two separate
pocket sections
for slashed pocket

On quality garments, the underpocket is cut from the fashion fabric or from lining and an additional piece of fashion fabric—a self-fabric *underpocket facing* at the top of the underpocket which prevents the lining fabric from showing when the pocket is used. This is particularly important when the opening isn't covered with a flap. The underpocket facing can be applied over the underpocket or seamed to it but the size remains about the same.

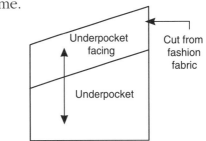

When planning the pocket sacks, consider the fabric weight and bulk, as well as the amount of fashion fabric available. Lightweight fabrics can be used for the entire sack, but to avoid bulk, heavier fabrics should be used with discretion. Here you can see how many fabric/lining combinations there are for pockets without flaps.

1. Self-fabric—one underpocket and one upper pocket.

2. Self-fabric—all-in-one pocket bag.

3. Self-fabric—one underpocket; lining—one upper pocket.

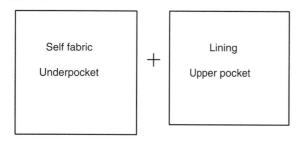

4. Self-fabric—facing; lining—all-in-one pocket sack with the facing *applied* to pocket bag at one end or near the center.

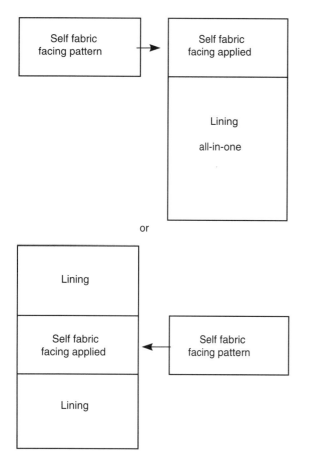

5. Self-fabric—facing; lining—all-in-one pocket with facing *seamed* to pocket bag.

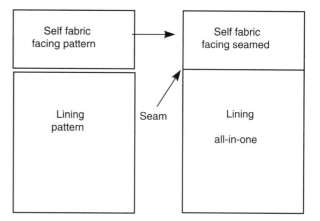

6. Self-fabric—facing; lining—one upper pocket and one underpocket with facing *applied* to top of underpocket.

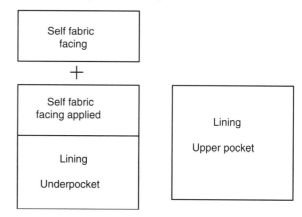

7. Self-fabric—facing; lining—one upper pocket and one underpocket with facing *seamed* to top of underpocket.

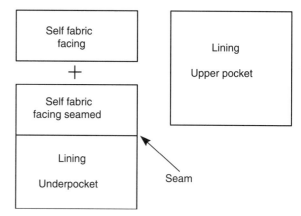

When making pockets with flaps, the self-fabric facing on the underpocket is sometimes eliminated to save time.

These directions are for a pocket sack with a separate underpocket and upper pocket. Generally, the underpocket is 1/4" to 1" longer than the upper pocket, depending on the size of the opening. The underpocket can have an applied or seamed facing.

1. On the paper pattern, outline the pocket opening the way it will look on the outside of the garment.

2. Using a colored pencil or line of dashes, draw the stitching line for the pocket sack (which you will see only from the inside of the garment). Round the corners at the bottom. Draw the pocket depth 3" to 10", depending on the design, location, and use.

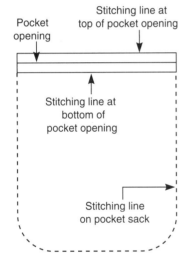

Stitching line at top of pocket opening

Pocket opening

Stitching line at bottom of pocket opening

Stitching line on pocket sack

Use colored pencil to outline pocket sack

The pocket sack on *bodices* should be 3" to 4" deep; on *skirts*, 5" or 6" ; *ladies' jackets*, 5" to 6"; *men's jackets*, 6" to 8" ; and *coats* 8" to 10" deep. To avoid bulk, it should not extend into the hem area.

Shape the sack so the pocket will hang well. On vertical pockets, the sack can be centered under the pocket opening or toward the garment center. If the opening is slanted, draw the edges of the sack parallel to the garment center. For added strength, extend the pocket sack so it will be sewn into a horizontal seam above it or into a side seam.

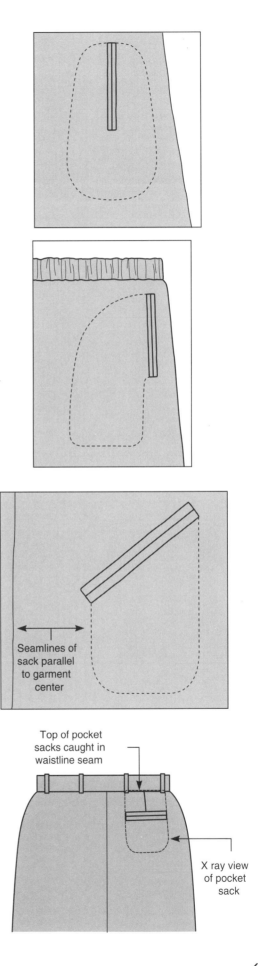

Seamlines of sack parallel to garment center

Top of pocket sacks caught in waistline seam

X ray view of pocket sack

Using a different colored pencil or solid line, add seam allowances to the pocket sack outline. In these directions seam allowances on the sides and bottom are the traditional 5/8" used by pattern companies, but the seam allowance at the top of the pocket is only 1/4".

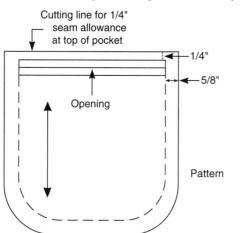

Indicate the grainline parallel to the garment section or garment center.

Hint: *I put the pattern paper under the garment pattern and use a stiletto tracing wheel to trace the sack.*

3. For the underpocket pattern, trace the stitching lines at the top of the opening and on the pocket sack. Add 1/4" seam allowance at the top and 5/8" on the remaining edges. Indicate the grainline.

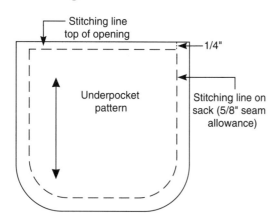

4. For the upper pocket pattern, trace the stitching line at the bottom of the pocket opening and on the pocket sack. Add a 1/4"

seam allowance at the top of the upper pocket and 5/8" seam allowance on the remaining edges. Indicate the grainline.

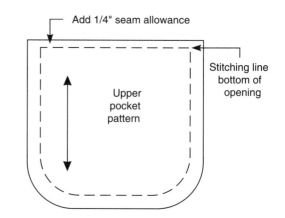

5. Use the underpocket pattern to make the facing pattern. Draw a line 3" – 4" below the top of the pattern, and indicate the grainline.

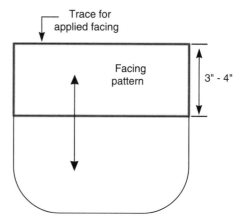

Begin with underpocket pattern

For an *applied facing*, trace the facing pattern to the drawn line.

For a *seamed facing*, cut the underpocket pattern on the drawnline. Add a 1/4" seam allowance to each section.

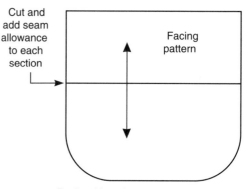

Begin with underpocket pattern

Pattern Development for All-in-One Sack:

Generally the all-in-one pocket sack is used only on horizontal pockets. Otherwise, the underpocket sack doesn't duplicate the grain of the garment and the pocket doesn't always hang properly.

1. Outline the pocket opening and sack on the garment pattern as described on page 46.

2. Fold a piece of pattern paper in half horizontally. Align the folded edge with the top of the opening or the bottom of the pocket sack. Trace the pocket sack and grainline. Add seam allowances as needed.

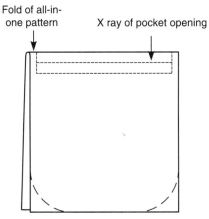

Align fold with top of sack

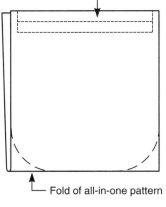

Align fold with bottom of sack

Pattern Changes for Commercial Patterns

When using a commercial pattern, I prefer to redesign the all-in-one pocket sack into two pieces. On the slash line midway between the two stitching lines, cut the pattern into two sections. Mark the top section "Underpocket" and the bottom section "Upper pocket."

Discard the pattern for the welts.

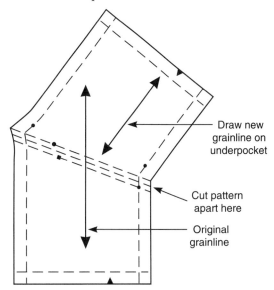

Sewing Notes:

1. Reinforce the pocket area with a pocket stay or interfacing to support the weight of the pocket and reinforce the pocket corners so they don't pull out when the pocket is used (see page X). When the garment section is underlined or backed, additional interfacing may not be needed, depending on the pocket location, the desired durability, and the underlining material grain.

Located under the pocket opening on the wrong side of the garment, the interfacing is cut with the lengthwise grain parallel to the opening. Generally it is about 3" wide and 2" longer than the opening.

With the garment section wrong side up, identify the pocket location and center the interfacing over the opening. Baste or fuse the interfacing in place.

Hints: *When using a fusible, test to be sure it won't have a shadow or demarcation line at the interfacing edges and that it won't bleed through to the right side.*

Experiment with different fusibles and/or pink the edges of the interfacing to prevent a demarcation line.

When the fashion fabric ravels badly and the demarcation line can't be avoided, use a fusible underlining on the entire section or use a narrow 1"-wide fusible stay.

2. Mark the pocket opening.

On some commercial patterns, the stitching lines—not the mouthline or slash—are indicated on the pattern, but many construction techniques use the mouthline as a guide. Determine at the outset which guide you will use, the mouthline or stitching lines, and mark the opening accordingly.

Hints: *To mark accurately, use the pattern as a guide. Mark the opening on the interfacing or wrong side of the garment with a temporary marking pen, tracing wheel and dressmaker's tracing carbon, tailor's tacks, or thread tracing.*

When using a commercial pattern, Nancy Zieman photocopies the section of the pocket pattern which has the stitching lines for the pocket opening. Then she pins the photocopy to the pocket lining, matching the dots, and stitches. The photocopy acts as a stabilizer and also gives an accurate stitching line.

Mark the mouthline, sometimes called the pocket placement line, carefully. Extend it beyond each end about 1-1/2". Mark the ends precisely with vertical lines 1" to 1-1/2" long.

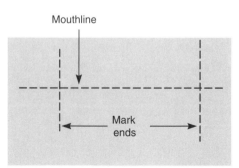

Mouthline

Mark ends

Hint: *On pockets set at an angle, the ends may be parallel to the garment center, not perpendicular to the opening. To avoid a major disaster, check before slashing to be sure the ends are marked and stitched accurately.*

Transfer the marked lines to the right side of the garment section with thread tracing, chalk, temporary marking pen, or machine basting.

Hint: *When using a sew-in interfacing, I prefer thread tracing because it also holds the layers together so they won't slip during the construction process. But I frequently use chalk or a soap sliver when using a fusible. I rarely use temporary marking pens on the right side because they occasionally stain permanently. Machine basting is my least favorite. It takes too long to remove and can leave needle holes.*

Before proceeding, examine the marked lines to be sure they are the correct length and are placed correctly. When sewing paired pockets, check to be sure they are identical in size and placement before slashing.

3. Review the Sewing Notes for the pocket you have selected. Interface any welts and baste the welts in place.

Note: *In the Sewing Notes for the Basic Slash Pocket, there are no instructions for sewing the pocket opening. However, double-welts are often illustrated, and sometimes mentioned as in this step, so that you can understand the relationship of the individual parts to the entire process. The double-welt pocket is shown because it it the most popular slash pocket.*

Hint: *To ensure accuracy, keep the welts from slipping by hand basting the stitching lines. Examine the pocket before stitching to be sure the length, width, and nap are correct.*

4. Stitch the opening.

Hint: *To stitch accurately, use a foot that holds the layers firmly and allows you to see the entire stitching line. Feet such as the straight stitch, clear plastic, zipper, or jeans foot are generally better choices than* the all-purpose zigzag foot. The zigzag foot has a bar at the front that obscures the marked points and lines, making it difficult to stitch precisely. The all-purpose, open-toed, and appliqué feet don't hold the fabric layers as securely.

For a strong seamline, shorten the stitch length to 20 stitches/inch or 1.25mm. An added advantage of a short stitch is that if you're one stitch off, it won't be noticed. Begin and end with a spottack, or a backstitch, or by tying the thread ends. Press.

Hints: Frequently a spottack isn't secure enough. To prevent the threads from pulling out at the end, pull the thread ends to the wrong side, give them a sharp tug, and knot them. I use a calyx-eyed needle to pull the thread ends through quickly and easily.

Another technique which works well on pockets is to begin stitching about 1/4" from the end. Stitch to the end. Pivot 180°. Stitch to the other end. Pivot again and stitch back 1/4".

5. If you're stitching a pair of pockets, stitch the second pocket. Before cutting, examine the work wrong side up to be sure the stitching lines are parallel and that they begin and end precisely. Check to be sure thread ends are fastened securely and that paired pockets are identical.

6. Slash the pocket opening.

Wrong side up, cut only the garment section without cutting into the welts. Beginning at the center, stop 1/2" from the ends. Clip diagonally *to-but-NOT-through* each corner, making a triangle or tongue at each end.

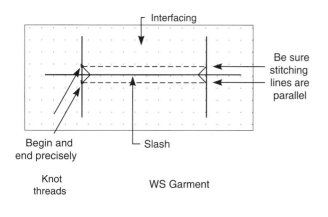

7. To turn the opening right side out, begin with the garment right side up and push any welts through the opening. Straighten them so they fill the opening as designed. Use a diagonal basting stitch to baste the opening closed.

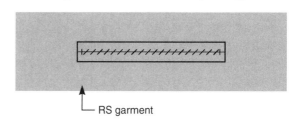

8. Press the opening with the garment section face down on a thick towel or a needle board. Press the back of the opening lightly with the point of the iron.

Hint: When pressing wool, cover the pressing surface with a wool press cloth or self-fabric to avoid flattening the fabric.

9. Secure the ends of the opening. Begin with the garment section right side up. Fold the garment edge and interfacing back to expose the triangle and welt ends. Using a short stitch and a zipper foot, stitch across the welt end as closely as possible to the fold of the garment. Repeat on the other end and press.

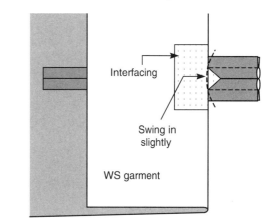

Hints: *On pockets that are more decorative than utilitarian, I stitch only once and swing in a tiny bit at the corners to catch all the cut threads. Too much swing will make a pleat. On pockets that will be used extensively, stitch across the triangle several times to strengthen it.*

On very fine garments and fragile fabrics, I sew first from the right side using a small fell stitch and matching thread. Sometimes, if the pocket is only decorative, I fell stitch the ends permanently from the right side instead of machine stitching.

10. Cut the pocket facing and sew it to the underpocket. When the underpocket is cut from self-fabric or when the pocket has a flap, it may NOT need a facing, but when it is cut from lining fabric or pocketing (a fabric used for pocket sacks), the lining frequently shows when the pocket is used. You can easily avoid this by sewing a facing to the underpocket.

In Method One that follows, the facing is applied to the top of the underpocket. In Method Two, it is seamed to the underpocket. In both methods the facing is cut from self-fabric so that the fabric design and/or nap duplicates the garment section.

11. After the pocket opening is completed, begin with the garment wrong side up to stitch the pocket sacks in place. Cover the back of the pocket opening with the upper pocket. The pocket is upside-down and face down against the wrong side of garment. Match and pin the raw edges at the bottom of the opening to the upper pocket.

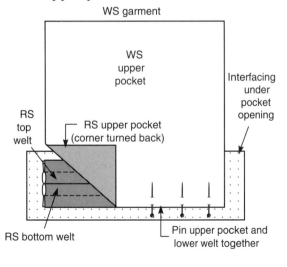

WS garment

WS upper pocket

Interfacing under pocket opening

RS top welt

RS upper pocket (corner turned back)

RS bottom welt

Pin upper pocket and lower welt together

Sidebar

Method One: Applied Facing

This method is a better choice for frequently used pockets and less durable fabrics, but it may be too bulky.

Use the underpocket pattern to cut the lining. Cut the top of the facing 3" - 4" long. Right sides up, match and baste the top of the facing to the top of the underpocket. Sew the bottom of the facing in place in the following way:

On *everyday garments*, zigzag the bottom over the raw edge.

For a clean finish on *lightweight materials*, fold the facing edge under and edgestitch it in place.

On *heavier fabrics*, serge the raw edge or cover it with seam tape.

On *better garments*, secure the edge with a catchstitch.

Hint: *Before continuing, check to be sure the nap or directional design on the facing duplicates the garment section.*

If you are using the all-in-one sack provided by the pattern company, mark the vertical centers of the pocket sack and facing. Right sides up, match and pin them together. Sew the top and bottom of the facing to the pocket sack.

Method Two: Seamed Facing

This method is suitable for firmly woven fabrics and pockets which will be used a moderate amount.

Make the underpocket facing and underpocket patterns.

Cut a self-fabric facing and a lining sack. Right sides together, join the facing and sack with a 1/4" seam. Press the seam toward the bottom of the pocket and understitch, if needed.

Then, with the garment section right side up, fold the garment back to expose the pinned seamline at the bottom of the pocket opening; stitch again on the original seamline. Repeat to sew the underpocket to the top of the opening.

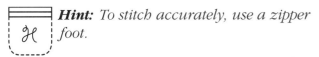 ***Hint:*** *To stitch accurately, use a zipper foot.*

In the diagram, you can see the stitched line on the underpocket from the wrong side of the garment.

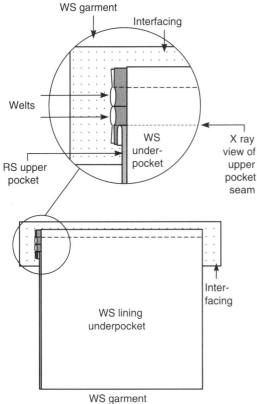

12. If the design has a buttonhole below the opening, complete the buttonhole on the garment before finishing the pocket sack.

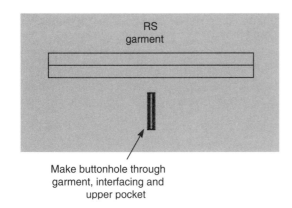

Make buttonhole through garment, interfacing and upper pocket

Wrong side up, smooth and baste the upper pocket flat against the garment. Turn the section over and mark the buttonhole location about 1/2" – 1" below the pocket opening.

Machine stitch the buttonhole.

13. To complete the pocket sack, first smooth the pocket bags and pin them together. Stitch the sides and bottom, catching the triangular ends.

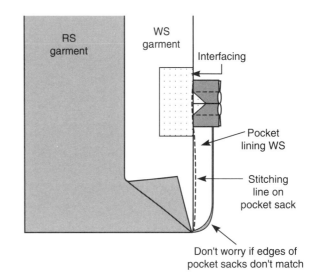

Don't worry if edges of pocket sacks don't match

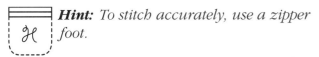 ***Hints:*** *If the raw edges don't match exactly, don't worry. You can always stitch a smaller seam if needed and trim the longer bag. But if you make them match, the pocket sacks may pull or ripple.*

To prevent the opening from gaping, hold the underpocket taut when pinning.

Grade the seam allowances. Above the opening, trim the welt to 1/2". Trim the underpocket to 1/4". At the ends of the welt, reduce bulk by rounding the corners and trimming away excess fabric. On unlined garments, trim a sew-in interfacing close to the pocket opening so the edges won't curl. Or use a catchstitch to sew the interfacing edges to the underlining or wrong side of the garment, keeping the catchstitches loose so they won't show on the right side of the garment.

Right side up, reinforce the ends of the pocket opening if it will be used extensively.

Hints: *On casual designs, jackets, vests, slacks, and other garments which will receive hard wear and on less-expensive sport fabrics, machine stitch triangles or bartacks at the ends.*

On finely tailored designs, fine fabrics, dresses, slacks, and quality suits, reinforce the corners with hand-stitched triangles, hand-stitched bartacks, or fell stitches. Well-made arrowheads are also attractive on some designs, but they are more fashionable some years than others.

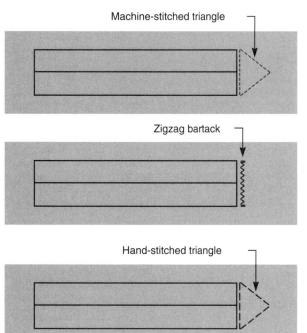

Machine-stitched triangle

Zigzag bartack

Hand-stitched triangle

To support the pocket weight, catchstitch the top of the pocket sack to the interfacing or underlining.

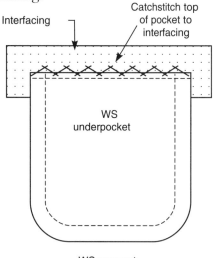

Interfacing

Catchstitch top of pocket to interfacing

WS underpocket

WS garment

Hint: *On pockets which will be used frequently, like those on men's jackets, use a stay of firmly woven interfacing or twill tape to support the pocket. Sew one end to the top of the pocket and the other to the armscye seam allowance.*

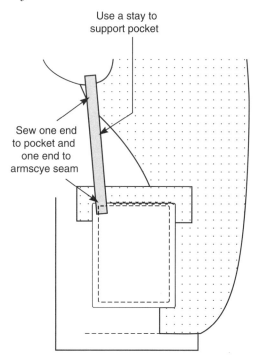

Use a stay to support pocket

Sew one end to pocket and one end to armscye seam

14. Press the pocket. Place the pocket over a ham right side up, and steam press using a self-fabric presscloth.

15. Remove all basting when the garment is finished.

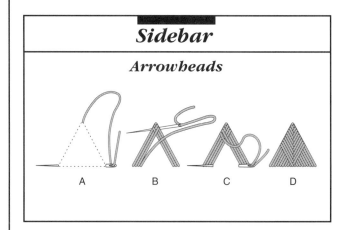

Sidebar

Arrowheads

A   B   C   D

Design Ideas for Slash Pockets

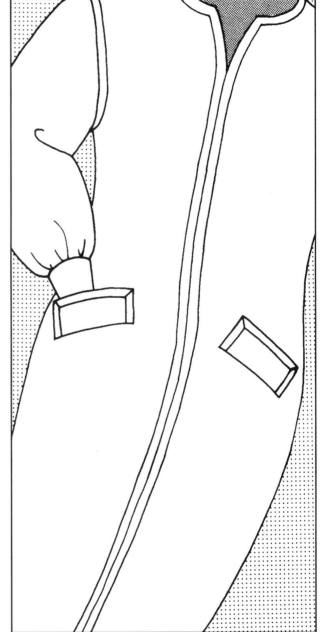

Frequently used on solid-colored fabrics, slash pockets can be plain and set on the crossgrain or fancy and set at a figure-slimming angle.

5. Porthole Pockets

Popularized by Pierre Cardin in the sixties, the porthole pocket was also a favorite of Coco Chanel. These were hidden under the flaps on her famous suits. It is the simplest slash pocket and easy to make. It is equally appropriate for elegant tailored designs and cute children's wear. You can let your imagination run wild when you create your designs.

The Porthole Pocket can be open to expose the pocket facing below it, or filled with a zipper, a single welt, or double welt strips.

The Basic Porthole Pocket is usually oval or rectangular in shape. It can also be round, triangular, or a novelty design. The exposed pocket facing can match the pattern of the garment fabric in design and grain, it can be a contrasting material, or it can be cut on a different grain.

Basic Porthole Pocket

Design Analysis:

These directions are for a pocket with a simple rectangular opening. The upper pocket is the facing for the opening, and the underpocket, which is exposed under the opening, is an integral part of the pocket design.

When designing for children, consider lips or heart and flower designs with contrasting underpockets to delight the wearers.

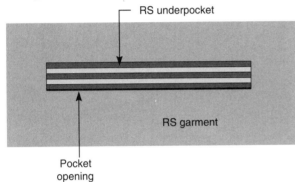

— RS underpocket

RS garment

Pocket opening

Pocket Development:

1. Review the Pattern Development for the Basic Slash Pocket on page 46.

2. Outline the pocket opening.

3. Make a pattern for the underpocket.

Sewing Notes:

1. Review the Sewing Notes for the Basic Slash Pocket on page 51 and the Magic Window Pocket on page 75.

2. For each pocket, cut one underpocket of self- or contrast fabric, according to the garment design. Cut the upper pocket using the underpocket pattern from lightweight self- or lining fabric, silk organza, cotton or blend organdy, or Sewin' Sheer.

3. Mark the pocket opening and interface the pocket area.

Hint: *Generally, I outline the pocket on the right side of the garment section; however, the upper pocket which faces the opening must be transparent enough to let you see the marks.*

4. Right sides together, pin or baste the upper pocket to the garment section so the top of the pocket sack extends above the opening 1/2".

5. Using a short stitch length (20 stitches/inch or 1.25 mm), stitch around the opening. Press.

Hints: *When you reach the beginning, overlap the stitches 1/4".*

For complex designs, make a template for the opening from a file folder or freezer paper. When outlining on the wrong side, work with the template face down. When using freezer paper, position the template on the upper pocket, dull side up. Press lightly so it will adhere to the surface.

6. Cut out the opening, trimming the seam to 1/8". Clip as needed so the seamline will be smooth when the upper pocket is turned to the inside.

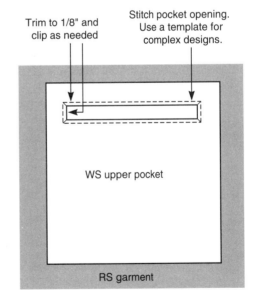

Trim to 1/8" and clip as needed

Stitch pocket opening. Use a template for complex designs.

WS upper pocket

RS garment

7. Turn the upper pocket to the wrong side, and with the garment wrong side up, press the upper pocket away from the opening.

8. Understitch the pocket. If the opening is a rectangle, understitch the long sides of the pocket, then understitch the ends. Press again, if needed.

Hint: *If you understitch around the pocket without breaking the threads at the corners, the facing will show at the corners. I stitch the two long edges first, then the short ones.*

9. Continuing wrong side up, cover the opening with the underpocket, and pin the edges of the pocket sacks together.

10. Right side up, fold back the garment and interfacing. Stitch on or close to the original seamline at the top of the pocket. Join the sides and bottom.

Variation: All-in-One Porthole

Design Analysis:

On this pocket, the underpocket and upper pocket sacks are cut all-in-one piece. This method eliminates a step and some of the bulk at the bottom of the pocket. It is suitable for horizontal pockets and light- to medium-weight fabrics.

Pattern Development:

1. Review the directions for the Basic Slash Pocket on page 46 and the Basic Porthole Pocket on page 59 and make the following changes.

2. To make the underpocket pattern, begin with a piece of pattern paper folded horizontally. Outline the underpocket on the folded paper with the fold at the bottom of the pocket sack.

3. Cut one pocket sack from self- or contrasting fabric.

4. Complete the pocket.

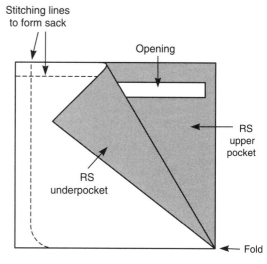

Stitching lines to form sack

Opening

RS upper pocket

RS underpocket

Fold

WS garment

Variation: Circle Porthole

The Circle Porthole can be any size and the underpocket can be cut from self- or contrasting fabric.

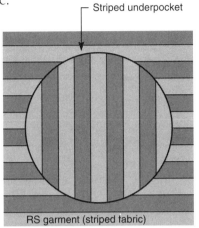

Striped underpocket

RS garment (striped fabric)

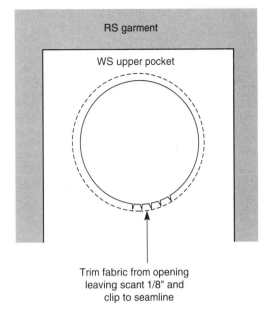

RS garment

WS upper pocket

Trim fabric from opening leaving scant 1/8" and clip to seamline

Sewing Notes:

1. Review the directions for the Basic Porthole Pocket on page 59 and make the following changes.

2. When stitching circles, use a short stitch for a stronger, smoother stitched line. To stitch a perfect circle, first tape a thumb tack to the machine. To mark the thumb tack location, measure to the right of the needle one-half the diameter of the circle. Tape the tack in place with the point up. Place the center of the circle on the tack, lower the foot, and stitch.

3. Trim away the excess fabric in the opening, leaving a scant 1/8" seam. Clip as needed so the facing will turn smoothly.

4. To join the pocket sacks, turn the garment wrong side up with the underpocket face down. Align and pin the raw edges of the underpocket and upper pocket. Turn the garment right side up and fold it back. Using the seamline around the opening as a guide,

stitch the pocket sack together at the top of the pocket opening, beginning and ending at the widest part of the opening.

5. Stitch the bottom of the pocket sack together with slightly rounded corners.

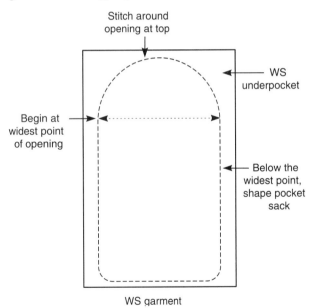

Stitch around opening at top

Begin at widest point of opening

WS underpocket

Below the widest point, shape pocket sack

WS garment

Variation: Porthole With a Zipper

The Porthole With a Zipper can be made with traditional pocket sacks or it can be made with just an underpocket topstitched flat against the garment. The zipper can be set by three different methods: edgestitching the faced opening, invisibly stitching the faced opening, and using the unfaced window.

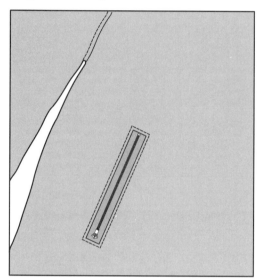

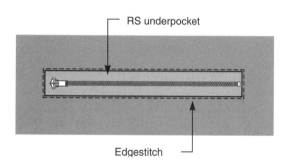

RS underpocket

Edgestitch

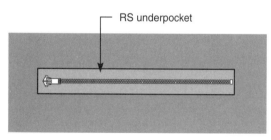

RS underpocket

Sewing Notes:

Review the Sewing Notes for the Basic Porthole Pocket on page 59.

Method One:
Face and Edgestitch

The edgestitched Porthole is the easiest. Cut the upper pocket from a lightweight lining material, and make the porthole. Center the zipper in the opening. Edgestitch it in place.

Method Two:
Face and Stitch Invisibly

The invisibly stitched Porthole is only slightly more difficult. Make the porthole. Glue- or fuse-baste the zipper into the opening. Then, with the garment right side up, fold the garment down to expose the seamline at the top of the opening that joins the garment and facing. Stitch again on the seamline. Repeat for the seamline at the bottom, then stitch the ends and press.

Hint: When stitching invisibly, use a zipper foot so you can stitch smoothly next to the zipper.

Method Three:
Unfaced

Slightly more difficult, the unfaced window has the least bulk but it is unsuitable for fabrics that ravel. Outline the finished opening on the interfacing side of the garment. Using a short machine stitch, reinforce the corners for 1/2" on each side. Slash the opening, and with the garment wrong side up, fold the cut edges back and press. Glue- or fuse-baste the zipper to the seam allowances and edgestitch or invisibly stitch it in place.

Design Ideas for Porthole Pockets

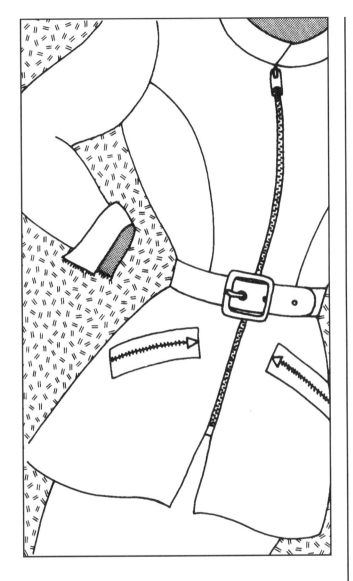

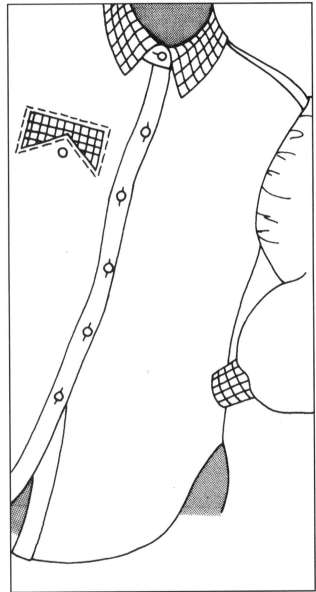

Well-suited for unusual opening shapes and exposed zippers, porthole pockets look great on casual funky designs, as well as crisp tailored garments.

6. Double-Welt Pockets

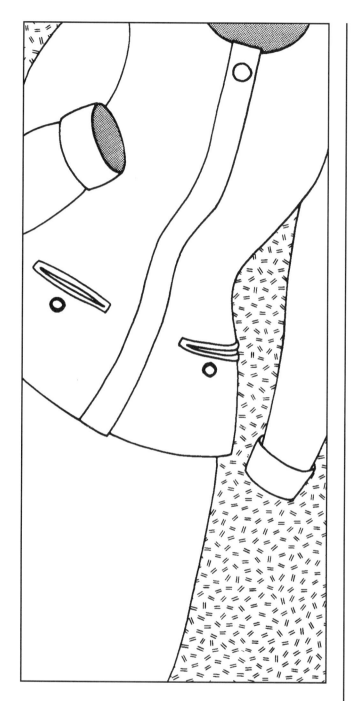

Double-welt pockets have many names: bound, piped, slashed, double-bound, double lip, buttonhole, tailored, besom, hacking, and jetted pockets. Made with two narrow welts, bindings, pipings, or lips at the opening, they look like large bound buttonholes. The besom-welt pocket has one narrow welt and one deep welt.

There are many different ways to make double-welt pockets, but depending on how they are made, all fall into two categories: bound or piped. *Bound pockets* are made by binding or wrapping the edges of the opening with separate strips, a patch, or the pocket sacks themselves, while *piped pockets* are made by sewing narrow strips to the pocket opening. When finished, they all look more or less the same from the outside of the garment. Unfortunately, neither method is suitable for all fabrics or for all pocket designs.

Depending on current fashion trends and the fabric, the binding or welts can be cut on the lengthwise grain, crossgrain, or bias. Bias welts are frequently used for solids, tweeds, and napped fabrics, and they are sometimes used on stripes and plaid fabrics to create special effects. On solid colors, pinstripes, herringbones, and boldly striped fabrics, welts are frequently cut with the lengthwise grain parallel to the opening, but they can also be cut to match the body of the garment.·

The opening on double welt pockets can be made by many different methods, but the five described in this book are most popular: the Strip method, the Bound method, the Patch method, the Five-line method, and the Magic Window method.

A. Strip Method

Design Analysis:

Used on luxury ready-to-wear, this is my favorite method for making welt pockets and bound buttonholes. It can be used on all firmly woven fabrics. The strips can be cut on the bias, lengthwise grain, or crossgrain, or they can be made of ribbon, braid, purchased or custom-made piping. On medium-weight fabrics, the welts are 1/4" – 1/2" deep so the finished pocket depth is 1/2" – 1". On light-weight fabrics the welts are frequently a little narrower, and on heavier fabrics, a little deeper, but they can be any width.

The pocket opening for this double-welt pocket is made by sewing two piping strips (welts) to the pocket opening. All seam allowances are pressed away from the opening. One of the advantages of this method is that vertical stripes and plaids, as well as printed patterns, can be matched, if desired.

Pattern Development:

1. Review the Pattern Development for the Basic Slash Pocket on page 46.

2. Outline the pocket opening on the pattern section. For these directions, the finished pocket opening is 6" wide and 1/2" deep; each welt is 1/4" deep and cut on the lengthwise grain. The pocket sack is 8" deep.

Draw the mouthline where the folded edges of the welts meet.

3. Make the pocket sack patterns or correct the commercial pattern (see page 51).

Sewing Notes:

1. Review the Sewing Notes for the Basic Slash Pocket on page 51.

2. For each pocket, cut an upper pocket and an underpocket. If the pocket doesn't have a flap and the fabric is light- or medium-weight, cut both sides of the pocket sacks from self-

fabric. If the fabric is heavy, cut a self-fabric facing so the underpocket won't show when the garment is worn and the pocket used.

Hint: When cutting an underpocket or pocket facing from a fabric with a bold pattern, nap or directional design, match it to the garment section.

Set aside self-fabric scraps or contrasting trim for the welts. The welts can be cut on any grain, but are generally cut on the lengthwise grain.

Hint: Donna Salyers likes to use Fabu-Leather for elegant welts. I also like Facile.

3. Interface the pocket area.

4. Mark the pocket mouthline on the right side of the garment section.

Hint: When sewing jackets with pockets at the hipline, Seattle designer Jane Whiteley redraws the mouthline with a hip curve so that it dips a scant 1/8" at the center of the opening. This subtle shaping helps eliminate pocket gaposis when the garment is worn.

5. Make the welts.

On bold, decorative stripes, match the welts to the garment section, select a color bar(s) which will be most attractive on the welt, or cut the welts on the bias. When cut on the bias, both welts can have the stripes chevron or continuous. When making a pair of pockets, all welts can be cut so the stripes are positioned from upper left to lower right or they can mirror each other.

When sewing pinstripes, locate the welt between two stripes so the welts are solid-colored. For large printed or woven patterns, match the welts to the fabric. For tweeds and napped fabrics, bias welts are attractive.

Press the welts, beginning with two fabric scraps which are at least 3" wide and 2" longer than the opening. Interface the welt strips if needed with a lightweight fusible or sew-in interfacing. Wrong sides together, fold each scrap on the lengthwise grain at least 1" from the edge. Press with steam.

Hint: *Working with a larger piece and trimming it after stitching is one of the industry secrets which Adeline Giuntini, a Berkeley, CA, tailor and my tailoring teacher at Laney College (a Peralta Community College) taught me. I never make a paper pattern for welts when using the Strip Method because it's impossible to fold a narrow strip lengthwise and press a sharp, straight fold without burning your fingers.*

Stitch a guideline on the welts a generous 1/4" from the folded edge. Trim the strip so the stitched line is a scant 1/4" from the edges—the stitched line will be almost in the center of the strip.

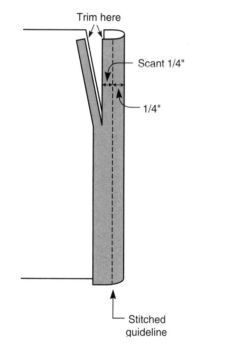

Trim here

Scant 1/4"

1/4"

Stitched guideline

Hints: *Stitch and trim accurately. If you trim too much, the welts will over lap; if you don't trim enough, there will be a gap between the welts.*

When you make your sample pocket, you may decide the width of the welts is too deep or too narrow for the fabric and pocket size. Generally, narrow welts are more attractive on lightweight fabrics, and wider ones are more attractive on heavy or bulky fabrics. Experiment with welts of different widths. You are the designer.

If you prefer, grade the strip so the two cut edges of the welt won't be on top of each other. Trim one layer to 1/4" and one to 1/2". Baste with the shorter layer next to the garment.

6. Baste the welts in place. Begin with the garment right side up. Align the cut edges of one welt strip with the mouthline so the welt ends extend at least 1" beyond each end of the mouthline. Baste precisely on the machine-stitched guidelines.

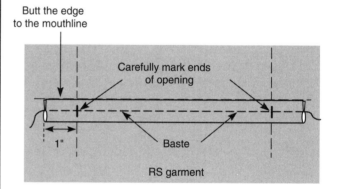

Butt the edge to the mouthline

Carefully mark ends of opening

1"

Baste

RS garment

Hints: *Carefully mark the ends of the opening on the welt strips with chalk, a soap sliver, or temporary marking pen.*

When matching plaids, stripes, or other fabric patterns, match the pattern at the stitching lines, not at the mouthline. Hand baste the welts in place. For most fabrics, I pin baste.

When sewing napped or directional design fabrics, fold the welts toward the mouthline before the final stitching to be sure the nap on the welts matches the nap on the garment.

7. Stitch the welts in place with the welt strip on top and the garment against the needle plate. Stitch next to the guideline, one thread nearer the fold. Position the other welt strip so the cut edges butt together. Baste and stitch.

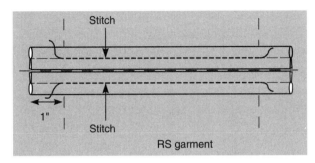

8. Wrong side up, examine the work to be sure the stitched lines are perfect and that patterns match. Fasten the thread ends securely. Slash the opening carefully to avoid cutting the welts.

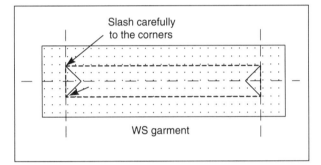

9. Right side up, push the welts through the opening. Straighten the welts so they fit into the opening properly.

Hint: Examine the welts. If they look limp or were cut on the bias, cord the welts so they won't stretch or gap. Thread a tapestry needle with acrylic or wool yarn and pull a double strand through the welt strips.

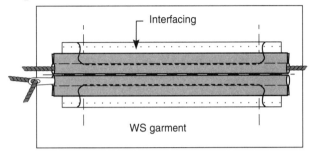

10. Baste the welts together with diagonal basting, and press the opening wrong side up.

11. Stitch the pocket sacks to the welt strips and complete the pocket. For complete instructions, see page 53, steps 7 – 15.

B. Bound Method

Design Analysis:

Used in haute couture, the Bound Method is well-suited for matching fabric patterns and for triangular and curved pockets. The Bound Method utilizes two flat fabric strips. When used on curves the strips are cut on the bias. When used on straight pockets, they are usually cut on the lengthwise grain or crossgrain.

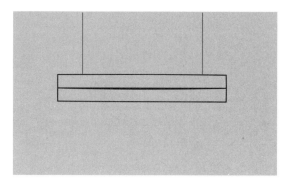

The differences between this method and the regular strip method are: the welts are easier to shape on a curved opening; the edges of the pocket are bound, not piped; the welt strips are not pressed or stitched before they are sewn to the garment; the strip at the top of the opening can be used for the pocket facing; the strip at the bottom of the opening can be used for the upper pocket; and, the pocket is more time-consuming to sew.

Pattern Development:

1. Review the Pattern Development for the Basic Slash Pocket on page 46.

2. Outline the pocket opening on the pattern section. For these directions, the finished pocket opening is 6" wide and 1/2" deep. The finished welts are 1/4" deep. The pocket bag is 6" deep.

3. Draw the pattern for the welts 2" wide and 2" longer than the finished opening. Indicate the grainline.

4. Make the pocket sack patterns or correct the commercial pattern (see page 51).

Sewing Notes:

1. Review the Sewing Notes for the Basic Slash Pocket on page 51.

2. For each pocket, cut two welts from self-fabric or contrast fabric. Bias-cut welts are easier to shape on curved pockets, but they may not be as attractive on patterned fabrics.

Hint: When matching patterns, match the stitching lines at the top and bottom of the opening, not the mouthline.

Cut the pocket sacks and a self-fabric pocket facing if needed.

3. Interface the pocket area.

4. Mark the pocket mouthline on the right side of the garment section. If the pocket opening isn't straight, mark the stitching lines also.

5. Shape the bias strips. Beginning wrong side up, press and stretch the bias strips to shape the strips to fit the pocket opening.

Hint: If the pocket is curved, one of the two welt strips will need to be longer than the other.

6. Right sides together, align the top edge of the lower welt with the mouthline. Hand baste 1/4"—the depth of the welt—from the raw edge, beginning and ending at the ends of the pocket opening. Repeat for the upper welt. Then, using chalk or a soap sliver, carefully mark the ends of the pocket opening on the welt. Machine stitch on the basted lines and fasten threads ends securely.

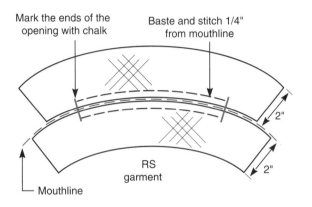

Shape strips to fit opening

Mark the ends of the opening with chalk

Baste and stitch 1/4" from mouthline

2"

2"

RS garment

Mouthline

Hint: Check your work before proceeding. If you are matching patterns, check to be sure they match.

7. Wrong side up, slash midway between the stitched lines and clip to the corners, without cutting the strips. Press the interfacing away from the slash. Trim the seam allowances in the opening to 1/16".

8. Push the strips through the opening and wrap them around the raw edges. Baste in the well of the seam.

Check to be sure the welt widths and folded edges are even and that the edges don't lap or gap at the center.

Hints: If the welts lap at the center, remove the basting and trim the seam allowances in the pocket opening a little more.

If the welts are too thick, remove the basting and press one of the seam allowances in the opening away from the slash.

9. Baste the welts together and secure the triangles at each end.

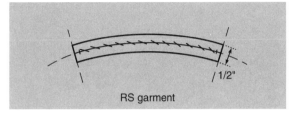

1/2"

RS garment

10. Secure the welts at the top and bottom of the opening. To duplicate the finish used in fine ready-to-wear, finish the long edges like the ends. Begin with the garment right side up. Fold the garment and interfacing back to expose the seam allowances and stitch again on the original seamline.

Hints: For a quick durable finish, ditch-stitch by machine. Begin with the garment right side up, and stitch on the seamlines at the top and bottom of the opening.

For a couture finish, use a fine silk thread and a tiny running stitch to ditch-stitch.

11. Press the pocket opening wrong side up.

Hint: Place a needle board or Velva-board under the pocket so you can press without leaving imprints. When pressing wool, cover the pressing surface with self-fabric to avoid crushing the wool.

12. Stitch the pocket sacks to the welt strips and complete the pocket. For more complete information, see page 53, steps 7 – 15.

C. Patch Method

Design Analysis:

One of the simplest methods for a Double-Welt Pocket, the Patch Method is a true bound pocket. Made with a single fabric patch, a rectangle is first stitched to outline the pocket opening. Then after the opening is slashed, the raw edges of the slash are bound and enclosed by the patch. Generally, the patch is easier to shape when it is cut on the bias, but it can be cut on any grain.

The Patch Method is suitable for fabrics which fray badly, light- to medium-weight fabrics, and designs which have bias-cut welts. It cannot be used when you want to match the welts to the fabric pattern on the garment section. Another disadvantage is that since the ends of the opening are stitched when the patch is applied, the seamlines at the end sometimes show if the pocket has been made carelessly.

Pattern Development:

1. Review the Pattern Development for the Basic Slash Pocket on page 46.

2. When using a commercial pattern, discard the pattern sections provided and make the pocket sacks and welts using these directions.

3. Outline the pocket opening on the pattern. For these directions, the finished pocket opening is 6" wide and 1/2" deep; the finished welts are 6" long and 1/4" deep. The pocket sack is 6" deep.

4. Draw the pattern for the patch 4" long and 2" wider than the finished width of the pocket opening. Indicate the grainline.

5. Make the pocket sack pattern. These directions for a horizontal pocket describe an All-in-One sack. Use a pattern with separate sacks if the pocket is not horizontal or if you like them better.

On the pattern paper, outline the pocket sack pattern so it is 1-1/4" wider than the pocket opening and twice the pocket depth.

Sewing Notes:

1. Review the Sewing Notes for the Basic Slash Pocket on page 51.

2. For each pocket, cut one patch and one pocket sack. Cut the patch on the desired grain 4" long and 8" wide. Cut the pocket sack 7-1/4" wide (the pocket width plus 1-1/4") and 12" long (twice the pocket depth). Cut a pocket facing if needed.

3. Interface the pocket area and patch as needed.

4. With the wrong side up, carefully draw the pocket opening on the interfacing.

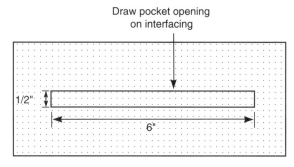

WS garment

Hint: *This rectangle must be stitched perfectly. Some stitchers use a template made from freezer paper, transparent tape, firm plastic, or graph paper.*

5. Right sides together, cover the opening with the patch so the patch is centered over the pocket opening. Pin or baste the patch in place.

Hint: *When using a bias patch, stretch the center of the patch so the finished welts will be taut and smooth.*

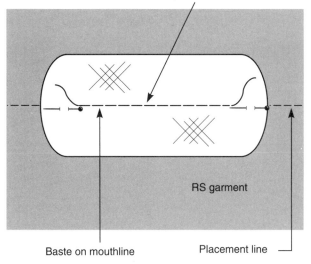

Stretch bias patch at center

RS garment

Baste on mouthline   Placement line

6. Wrong side up, stitch around the opening.

Hint: *When stitching pockets made by the patch method, begin at the center of one long side and stitch around the opening to make a rectangle. Shorten the stitch length as you approach each end. Carefully pivot at each corner and check to be sure you don't skip a stitch. Count the stitches at each end to be sure the ends will be even. Overlap the stitching 1/2" when you reach the beginning.*

7. Slash the pocket opening and patch. Then clip to the corners. Push the patch through the slash.

Hint: *Unless you used fusible interfacing, trim away the interfacing inside the triangle. I use appliqué scissors so I can trim close to the stitched line.*

8. Pull the patch sharply at the ends. Wrong side up, use the point of the iron to press the entire patch away from the opening. At this stage, the opening looks like a faced rectangle. Then release the patch and press the seamlines at the top and bottom of the opening so the long seam allowances fill the opening.

9. Hold the garment right side up, and wrap the patch around the seam allowances. Straighten the welts so they are even and fill the area within the stitched lines. Pin. Baste the welts together with a short diagonal basting stitch.

Hints: *If the welts form a peak at the center, unpin the welts and, wrong side up, trim the seam allowances 1/16".*

If the welts look too thick or bulky, unpin the pocket. Press the seams at the top and bottom open so only the welt seam allowances are in the opening.

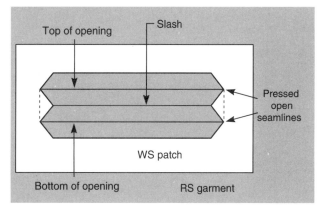

Top of opening   Slash

Pressed open seamlines

WS patch

Bottom of opening   RS garment

10. Ditch-stitch by hand or machine to secure the welts.

Hint: *Be sure the upper welt is sewn securely since the pocket pouch will hang from this seamline. If you pressed the seams open, fold back the garment and stitch again on the seamline.*

11. Stitch the triangles at the ends of the opening.

12. Press the pocket opening wrong side up.

13. Join one end of the pocket sack to the top of the patch. Repeat to join the bottom of the patch and the other end of the sack.

14. Stitch the sides of the pocket sack, catching the triangles at the ends of the opening. Catchstitch the top edge to the interfacing.

Variation: Deep Welts

The deep welt has a wider opening and deeper welts. Most have a 3/4" opening with 3/8" welts, but on novelty pockets the opening can be 1" – 2" deep.

Sewing Notes:

1. Review the directions for the Patch Method on page 70 and make these changes.

2. For a finished opening 6" wide and 1" deep, cut the patch 5" wide by 8" long and stitch the rectangle for the pocket opening 6" wide by 3/4" deep.

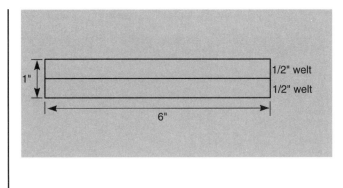

Variation: Besom-Welt

This design has a narrow welt (3/16") at the top and a deep welt (5/8") at the bottom. Frequently used on men's garments under a flap, the name "Besom-Welt" is used more frequently in the British Isles than in the United States.

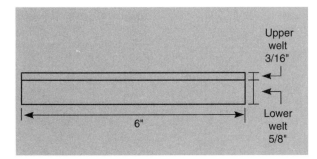

1. Review all the directions for the Patch Method on page 70 and make these changes.

2. For a finished opening 6" wide and 1" deep, cut the patch 5" wide by 8" long, and stitch the rectangle for the pocket opening 6" wide by 1" deep.

3. Carefully slash the opening so the slash is exactly 5/8" from the bottom of the opening.

Hint: Since the inside of the rectangle fills the welts, it must be cut precisely.

4. Turn the welts through to the wrong side and shape them so that the bottom welt is 5/8" and the top welt is 3/16". (For the math whizzes, the extra 1/16" is absorbed by the fabric layers.)

D. Five-Line Method

Design Analysis:

According to Edna Bryte Bishop, founder of the Bishop Method of Sewing and one of the authors of *Super Sewing* (1974), "when the steps...are carefully learned,...(this method) is virtually foolproof." It is included here because it is a favorite of many teachers and homesewers.

Originally called the One-Piece Tucked Strip Tailored Buttonhole, it was obviously designed for making bound buttonholes. Today it's generally called the Five-Line Method because it utilizes five stitching lines to form the welts. Since three of the lines are basting rows, it is not suitable for fabrics which are easily marred by machine needles. This is why it's not one of my favorites. However, if you use it and are pleased with the results, continue—the finished result is really the only thing that matters. And, if you don't use it now and aren't pleased with your results using other methods, try it.

Pattern Development:

1. Review the Pattern Development for the Basic Slash Pocket on page 46.

2. Outline the finished pocket on the pattern section. For these directions, the finished pocket opening is 6" wide and 1/2" deep. The finished welts are 1/4" deep on this design. The pocket bag is 6" deep.

> **Hint:** *If your fabric is medium to heavy, make the welts 3/8" deep.*

3. Draw the pattern for the welt patch 3" wide and 2" longer than the finished opening. Indicate the grainline parallel to the opening. The welts can be cut on any grain to enhance the design, but they are usually cut with the lengthwise grain or bias parallel to the opening.

4. Make the pocket sack patterns or correct the commercial pattern.

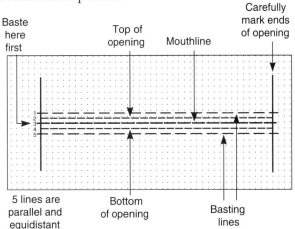

5 lines are parallel and equidistant

Sewing Notes:

1. Review the Sewing Notes for the Basic Slash Pocket on page 46.

2. For each pocket, cut one welt patch from self- or contrast fabric. Cut the pocket sacks and a self-fabric facing if needed.

3. Interface the pocket area and the welt patch, as needed.

4. Mark the pocket mouthline on the interfacing. Also, on the interfacing, use a very sharp pencil or fine marking pen to draw two parallel lines on both sides of the mouthline, spacing them 1/4" apart. Carefully mark the ends of the pocket opening.

> **Hint:** *If you can't mark the interfacing precisely, draw the guidelines on stabilizer, lightweight non-woven fusible interfacing, or 1/4" graph paper, and baste or fuse it to the interfacing.*

5. Right sides together, center and pin the welt patch over the opening.

6. Interfacing side up, machine baste on the mouthline and on the lines at the top and bottom (lines 1 and 5).

Check again after stitching the next two lines to be sure they are parallel and equidistant from the mouthline. If they aren't, the finished welts will be uneven and ugly. If the basting rows extend beyond the pocket opening, it won't affect the finished welts.

7. With the garment right side up, press the edges of the welt patch toward the mouthline, using a press cloth if needed. Pin in place.

8. Interfacing side up, stitch on one of the remaining guidelines (line 2 or 4). Check before stitching to be sure the welt will be smooth and that the other welt is held out of the way. Start and stop precisely at the ends of the pocket opening. On the right side, you have stitched one welt. Repeat on the remaining guideline to finish the welt.

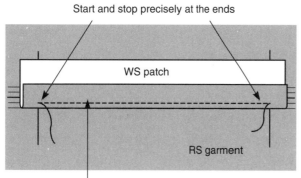

Start and stop precisely at the ends

WS patch

RS garment

RS patch

9. Fasten the thread ends securely and remove the basting. Remove the graph paper, if you used it.

10. Hold the top and bottom of the welt patch out of the way on the right side of the garment, and cut through only the welt patch at the center, all the way across the patch. Then slash the pocket opening and clip to the corners.

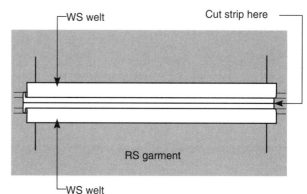

WS welt

Cut strip here

RS garment

WS welt

11. Pull the welt strips through to the back and baste the lips together. Stitch the ends of the triangles.

12. Press the pocket opening wrong side up.

13. Stitch the pocket sacks to the welt strips and complete the pocket. For more complete information, see page 53, steps 7 – 15.

E. Magic Window Method

Sometimes called a faced, windowpane, window, butterfly, or organza patch method, the Magic Window is very similar to the Porthole Pocket. The opening is made by finishing the opening with a facing instead of the upper pocket. Then the welt pipings are sewn in place behind the opening.

The Magic Window is suitable for a variety of fabrics, including plaids and stripes. It can be used for applied welt, novelty welt, porthole, zipper, and fake pockets, as well as bound buttonholes, besom welts, and decorative insets. The welts can be any depth from 3/16" – 1" but they are generally 1/4" – 3/8". The welts can be the same width top and bottom, the bottom welt can be deeper, or they can lap. And, since this method is very versatile, the pocket opening doesn't have to be a rectangle. It can be a circle, triangle, or novelty shape.

This home-sew method is very popular with many teachers because it's easy to teach and even inexperienced students can expect good results. But it's never used in the fashion industry. An astute observer can identify the technique and will label the garment "made at home."

Pattern Development:

1. Review the Pattern Development for the Slash Pocket on page 46.

2. Outline the finished pocket on the pattern section. For these directions, the finished pocket opening is 6" wide and 1/2" deep. The finished welts are 1/4" deep (half the pocket depth). The pocket bag is 6" deep.

Hint: When the Magic Window is used for a Besom-Welt Pocket, make the pocket window 3/4" deep, with the upper welt 1/4" and the lower welt 1/2". See page 75.

3. Draw the facing pattern 2" longer and 2" wider than the finished opening. Indicate the grainline.

4. Make the pattern for the welts 2" wide and 2" longer than the pocket width. Indicate the grainline.

Hint: If the welts are unusually shaped or deep, make the pattern twice the finished welt width plus 2".

5. Make the pocket sack patterns or correct the commercial pattern.

Sewing Notes:

1. Review the Sewing Notes for the Basic Slash Pocket on page 51.

2. For each pocket, cut two welts from self-fabric or contrast fabric.

Hint: When sewing casual designs, be creative. Replace the traditional self-fabric welts with contrast fabric, ribbon, ribbings, or serger-trimmed fabric welts. Tammy Young and Naomi Baker use decorative threads to serge-finish the welt edges. Experiment with stitch adjustments for length, width, and tension on fabric scraps before serging the pocket welts.

Cut the pocket sacks and a self-fabric facing, if needed. Cut the window facing from a lightweight facing fabric.

Hint: Generally I prefer natural-fiber materials such as silk organza or cotton batiste for the facing because they are easier to shape and they can be pressed sharply at the edges of the opening. I've also had good results with the nylon interfacing Sewin' Sheer. Generally, synthetic and permanent press fabrics are too resilient. Even though the color may match, the facing frequently shows at the corners.

3. Interface the pocket area and welts as needed.

4. Draw the pocket opening on the interfacing.

5. To make the welts, begin right sides together. Baste the welts together lengthwise at the centers. Open the welts so the right sides are out and press. Set the welts aside.

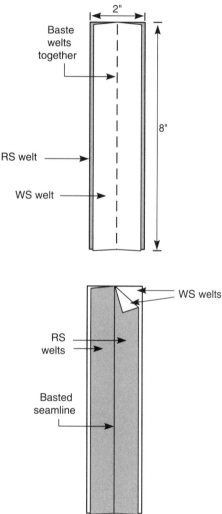

6. Right sides together, center the facing patch over the pocket opening. Pin or baste the patch in place.

7. Shorten the stitch length and stitch a rectangle around the opening.

8. Slash the pocket opening and facing and clip to the corners. Push the facing through the slash.

9. Wrong side up, adjust the facing so you can see the seam at the edges of the opening. Use the point of the iron to press the facing away from the opening.

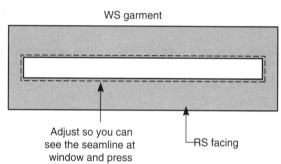

10. Understitch the long sides of the pocket; then understitch the ends. Press again, if needed.

11. Right sides up, position the welts under the opening. For a regular double-welt pocket, center them. For a besom-welt pocket, make the lower welt 1/2" and the upper welt 1/4".

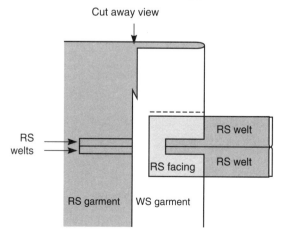

Hint: *Apply a basting aid like washable glue stick or a fusible web on release paper to the exposed edge of the facing. When using the fusible, cut two 1/4" wide strips the length of the welts.*

12. Right sides up, baste the welts in place.

Hint: *When fuse basting, begin right side up and cover the pocket with a press cloth. Some stitchers baste around the opening with a zigzag stitch. This is my least favorite method. It's as quick and easy to hand baste with a diagonal stitch. Then you're confident your welts won't slip and you won't be left with ugly needle holes.*

13. To secure the welts, begin right side up. To set the upper welt, fold the garment back to expose the seamline at the top of the opening. Stitch again on this seamline. Repeat for the lower welt.

Hint: *If the design is made in a luxury fabric or the pocket is just for looks, secure the welts by hand sewing the seamlines with a running stitch instead of machine stitiching or ditch-stitch the top and bottom by hand. On some fabrics such as tweeds and fabrics with texture, you can ditch-stitch invisibly by machine.*

14. Press the pocket opening wrong side up.

15. Stitch the pocket sacks to the welt strips and complete the pocket and remove all basting.

Variation: **Elizabeth's Million-Dollar Lips**

When College of the Desert teacher Elizabeth Lawson makes her million-dollar pocket, she uses a piece of lightweight fusible interfacing instead of an organza patch. First she sews the interfacing with the fusible side down so that when the facing is turned, the fusible will be exposed. After it's turned to the wrong side, she fuses the welts in place.

Hint: *To avoid getting the fusible on your iron, do NOT press the fusible with a bare iron. Use a Teflon pressing sheet or a discarded sheet of release paper from Wonder-Under.*

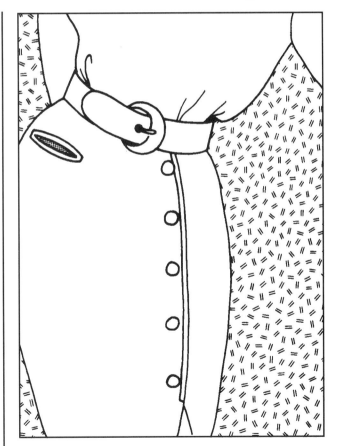

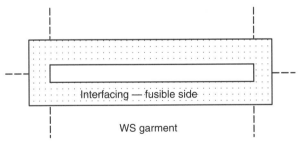

Interfacing — fusible side

WS garment

Variation: Non-Woven Fabrics

Design Analysis:

A variation of the Magic Window Method, this pocket can be made quickly and easily on nonwoven materials such as felts, synthetic suedes and leathers, and real leathers and suedes.

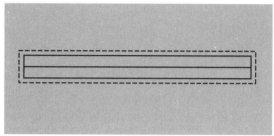

Sewing Notes:

1. Review the directions for the Magic Window Pocket and make the following changes.

2. Cut two welts 2" deep and 2" wider than the pocket opening. Cut a self-fabric facing if the threads. Open the welts so the right sides are out; press. Set the welts aside.

3. To make the welts, begin right sides together.

Beginning at one end, sew the welts together for 3/4". Repeat at the other end. Knot the threads. Open the welts so the right sides are out; press. Set the welts aside.

4. Outline the pocket opening on the garment so it is the exact size and shape of the finished opening.

5. Interface the pocket opening on the wrong side with self-fabric. Glue baste or fuse it in place.

6. Using a mat knife or small sharp scissors, cut out the opening.

7. If you're using interfacing, draw the window on the interfacing, and cut it away before fusing it. Trim another 1/8" away from the window so it won't show on the finished pocket. Then fuse the interfacing in place.

8. Right sides up, position the welts under the opening. Glue baste.

9. Set the welts permanently by edgestitching around the pocket opening from the right side of the garment.

Variation: James Dean Pocket

Made to duplicate the jacket James Dean wore in the movie *Rebel Without A Cause*, this Magic Window variation has two 1"-deep welts which are on top of each other and lap top over bottom. The pocket opening must be at least an inch longer than standard welt pockets because the overlapped welts make it more difficult to insert your hand. This is an excellent design for golf and fishing jackets when you want the pockets to hold small items securely.

1. Review the directions for the Magic Window Method on page 75 and make these changes.

2. Outline the pocket opening on the pattern section. For these directions, the finished pocket opening is 7" wide and 1" deep. Each of the finished welts is 1" deep. The pocket bag is 6" deep.

3. Draw the pattern for the welts 3-1/4" wide and 2" longer than the finished opening. Indicate the grainline.

4. To make the welts, fold and press each welt in half lengthwise, wrong sides together. Machine baste the long raw edges together, and press.

5. Face the pocket opening.

6. Right sides up, position the upper welt in the opening so that it fills the entire window, with the fold at the bottom. Baste and stitch the *top* of the opening.

Position the lower welt under the upper welt so that the fold is at the top of the opening. Turn the section wrong side up. Baste and stitch the *bottom* of the opening.

7. Stitch the ends and complete the pocket.

Design Ideas for Double-Welt Pockets

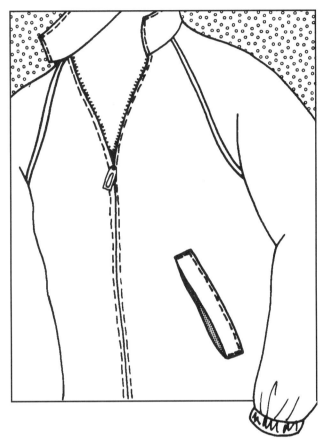

The most versatile of the slash pockets, double-welt pockets can be used on men's and women's garments. They are equally attractive when used alone or in pairs.

7. Single-Welt Pockets

Generally reserved for dressy garments and tailored designs, single-welt pockets are frequently used on skirts, blouses, suits, jackets, and trousers. Pockets can be made with the welt set into the opening or applied over it. They can have a welt that is the same size as the opening, a smaller welt which fills a portion of the opening, or a welt that is larger than the opening.

Single-welt pockets fall into two broad categories—set-in welts and applied welts. Set-in welts are made by stitching the welt into the opening on three sides. Applied welts are first finished at the top and ends, then applied to the garment surface over the opening. Because of this difference in the pocket construction, applied welt pockets are more pronounced than set-in welt pockets.

On single-welt pockets, the welt can be cut in one piece with the upper pocket sack or as a separate welt. The bottom of the opening can be finished with the welt, a facing, or an underpocket. The top is usually finished with a simple facing or the underpocket, but it can also have an added flap.

Unlike double welt pockets, which may have no interfacing in the welts, most single-welt pockets are interfaced so they will hold their shape.

Before making single-welt pockets on the garment section, consider the fabric weight, texture, and design, as well as the garment design, your sewing skills, time available, and personal preference, then experiment with several different methods.

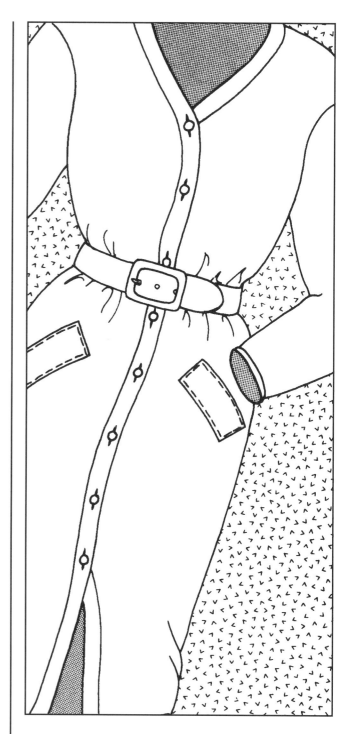

Set-in Welt Pockets—Two Construction Methods

Set-in welt pockets have many names—all-in-one welt pocket, the one-piece welt, separate welt, and single lip pockets. Made with a single wide welt that fills or almost fills the opening, set-in welts can be made by adapting many of the methods for double-welt pockets described in the previous section. But they all fall into two groups: the one-piece welt and the separate welt. The One-Piece Welt Pocket is made by cutting the welt all-in-one piece with the upper pocket, while the Separate Welt Pocket is made by cutting the welt and upper pocket in two sections. At first glance, all set-in welts look more or less the same, but the separate welt pocket is more versatile because the welt can be made from materials or cut on grains which are unsuitable for use on the upper pocket. The one-piece welt is generally flatter because there are fewer seam allowances at the bottom of the opening.

Either of these methods can be used with a flap. Generally on jackets and men's trousers, the flap is sewn into the seamline at the top of the pocket opening. But it can be applied by hand or machine to the garment surface to cover a less-than-perfect pocket. (See Appendix: Welts and Flaps.)

Method One: One-Piece Welt

Design Analysis:

Sometimes called an all-in-one welt pocket, the One-Piece Welt is cut from self-fabric in one piece with the upper pocket. When used on lightweight fabrics, it can even be cut in one with the underpocket so that one section forms the welt and the entire pocket sack.

Pattern Development:

1. Review the Pattern Development for the Basic Slash Pocket on page 46.

2. Outline the pocket opening on the pattern. For these directions, the finished pocket opening is 5" wide and 1/2" deep. The pocket sack is 5" deep.

3. Make the pattern for the welt/upper pocket 2" wider (7") than the pocket opening and 2" longer (7") than the pocket depth. Indicate the grainline.

Hint: Depending on the fabric and its design, the welt/upper pocket can be cut with the lengthwise grain parallel or perpendicular to the opening. An added advantage of the former is that the welt will hold its shape better, even though it may not be interfaced.

Make the pattern for the underpocket the same width (7") and 1" shorter (6"). Make a pocket facing if needed.

Sewing Notes:

1. Review the Sewing Notes for the Basic Slash Pocket on page 51.

2. Cut the pocket sections from the fashion fabric.

3. Interface the pocket area and the welt/upper pocket, as needed.

Hint: If the welt/upper pocket is cut on the bias, interface the entire section with a lightweight fusible cut on the grain. I use a 3/4"-wide strip of lightweight fusible and fuse it to the welt end of the upper pocket.

4. Mark the stitching lines of the pocket opening on the right side of the garment.

5. Right sides together, lap the top of the upper pocket (the longer sack that forms the welt) over the bottom of the opening 1/4". Baste at the bottom of the opening. Mark the ends of the opening. Stitch on the basting line, beginning and ending 1" from the raw edges—the width of the seam allowance. Knot the threads at the ends with knots. Repeat for the underpocket.

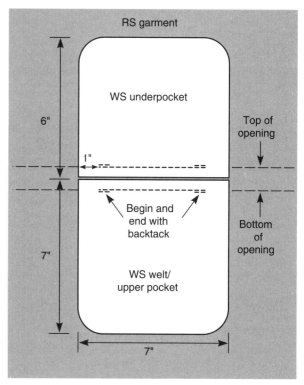

Hint: On this pocket the raw edges meet at the center of the pocket, but if the opening were deeper they would not. The stitched lines establish the top and bottom of the opening. When stitching, begin and end precisely at the ends of the opening, not at the edges of the seam allowances. After both pocket sacks are stitched, examine the wrong side. The stitched lines should be parallel and begin and end precisely.

6. Wrong side up, slash the pocket opening without cutting the welt or underpocket.

7. Right side up, press the welt/upper pocket toward the opening, then push both pocket sections through to the wrong side. Wrong side up, press the seam at the top of the opening away from the opening.

8. Right side up, arrange the upper pocket around the seam allowances at the bottom of the opening to form a 1/2"-wide welt. Straighten the ends of the welt inside the pocket opening.

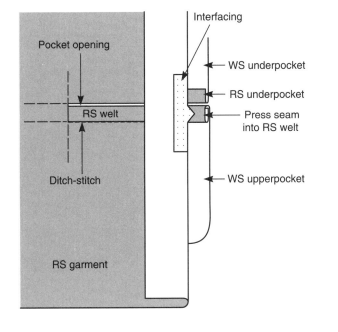

9. To secure the welt, ditch-stitch in the seam by hand or machine.

 Hint: *To secure the welt invisibly, press the seam at the bottom of the opening open. Then, right side up, fold the garment edge back to expose the seamline. Hold the underpocket out of the way. Stitch again on the seamline.*

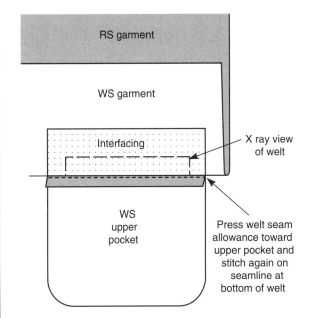

10. Stitch the triangles and welts at the ends.

 Hint: *For a more durable pocket on trousers, edge stitch around the pocket opening.*

11. Complete the pocket.

Method Two: Separate Welt

Design Analysis:

Like the One-Piece Welt Pocket, the Separate Welt Pocket is used on dresses, skirts, blouses, suits, jackets, and trousers. The welt fills the pocket opening, but since the welt is a separate section, it can be much more decorative. It can be made on a different grain, from another fabric, with serging at the edges, or from ribbing, ribbon, or braid.

Pattern Development:

1. Review the Pattern Development for the Basic Slash Pocket on page 46.

2. Outline the finished pocket on the pattern. For these directions, the finished pocket opening is 5" wide and 1" deep. The pocket sack is 5" deep.

3. Make the pattern for the welt 2" wider than the finished pocket opening and twice the finished depth plus 5/8". For a 5" by 1" opening, cut the welt 7" wide and 2-5/8" deep. If the welt fabric is heavy, make the pattern 2-3/4" deep to allow for the turn of the cloth.

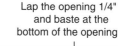 **Hint:** *If the welt is made of ribbon or braid, you won't need a pattern. But the ribbon should be 1/4" wider than the finished welt.*

4. Make the pocket pattern for the pocket sacks, and a facing if needed. The underpocket should be 6" longer to cover the 1" pocket opening.

Sewing Notes:

1. Review the Sewing Notes for the Basic Slash Pocket on page 51.

2. Cut the pocket sacks from self-fabric or lining. Cut a pocket facing from self-fabric, if needed.

3. Interface the pocket area and welt as needed.

4. Mark the pocket opening on the right side of the garment section. Then chalk mark a line inside the pocket opening at the top and bottom for a welt placement line.

5. Fold and press the welt, wrong sides together. Baste the ends.

6. With the garment right side up, lap the raw edges of the welt over the bottom of the opening by 1/4". Mark the ends of the opening on the welt. Baste 1/4" from the long edge so the edges of the welt are aligned with chalked line near the bottom of the opening.

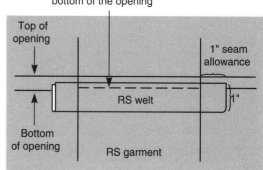

7. Continuing right side up, place the upper pocket face down on the welt and align the raw edge with the chalked line near the top of the opening. Stitch, beginning and ending 5/8" from the raw edges—the width of the side seam allowance. Knot the threads at the ends. Repeat for the underpocket.

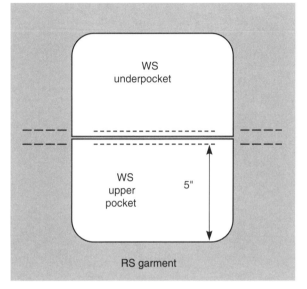

8. Wrong side up, slash the pocket opening. Push the pocket sacks through to the wrong side. Then, with the wrong side up, press all seams away from the opening.

9. Arrange the welt in the opening. Stitch the triangles and welts at the ends, and complete the pocket.

Applied Welt Pockets

Design Analysis:

Sometimes called a stand pocket, outside or tailored welt pocket, upturned or upright flap pocket, breast, handkerchief, or simply welt pocket, Applied Welt Pockets are closely related to flaps and patch pockets because they are applied elements that enhance the garment design.

This versatile pocket is particularly attractive on crisp fabrics, linen, silk and cotton suitings, wools, and brocades. It can be placed horizontally, vertically, or on a slant. It can be made from self-fabric or contrasting fabric, and even though the welt generally duplicates the grain and nap of the garment, it can be cut on a different grain. Applied Welts can be small or large, depending on the garment design, fabric, and pocket location, but generally larger welts are used on heavier fabrics, tailored designs, and pockets below the waist.

Sometimes considered the most difficult pocket to master, the Applied Welt requires the most concentration to sew successfully. When located on a slant, it is easy to stitch and cut the opening incorrectly. Actually, Applied Welt Pockets aren't difficult to sew, but you must *mark accurately, stitch precisely, and cut carefully.* They do require practice. When you consider that they are used only on more expensive ready-made garments because they are the most costly to make in fashion production, perfect pockets on your own garments are worth the time and practice required.

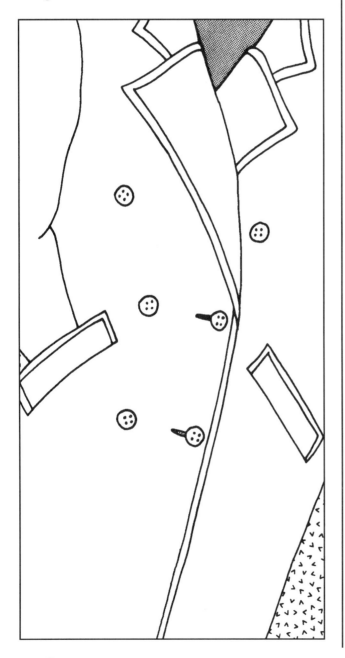

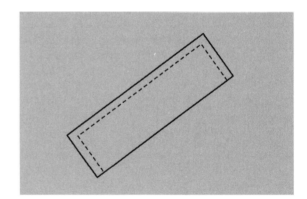

Pattern Development:

1. Review Pattern Development for the Basic Slash Pocket on page 46 and Appendix: Welts and Flaps on page 106.

2. Outline the welt on the garment pattern. The Applied Welt is frequently a rectangle or parallelogram with the ends parallel to the garment center. However, it can have a shaped edge.

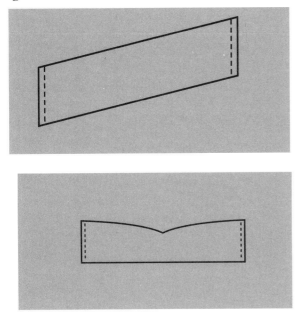

3. Trace the outlined welt, make the pattern for the welt and welt facing, and indicate grainlines.

Hint: Review Welt Applications starting on page 112 and decide how the welt ends will be secured. Then indicate any topstitching on the welt pattern.

4. Using a different colored pencil on the garment pattern, outline the slash and opening under the welt. At the top of the opening the finished welt should extend 1/4" to 1/2" beyond the opening at the top and 1/2" to 1" at the side beyond the top of the opening. The welt is the same size as the bottom of the opening.

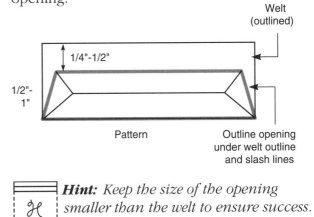

Welt (outlined)

1/4"-1/2"

1/2"- 1"

Pattern

Outline opening under welt outline and slash lines

Hint: Keep the size of the opening smaller than the welt to ensure success.

5. If the welt will be applied directly to the garment instead of sewn into the pocket opening, mark the welt placement line on the garment pattern.

6. Make the patterns for the pocket sacks.

7. Depending on the garment, welt design, and fabric, decide whether you will make a one-piece welt or a welt with a separate facing. Make the welt and welt facing patterns.

Sewing Notes:

1. Review the Sewing Notes for the Basic Slash Pocket on page 46 and Welts and Flaps on page 106.

2. Cut the pocket sacks from self-fabric or lining. Cut a pocket facing if needed. Cut the welt and welt facing.

3. Interface the pocket area and welt.

4. Mark the stitching lines on the garment with thread so you can see them on both sides of the garment. Mark the slash line with chalk or temporary marking pen.

Hint: Mark accurately—this is the most important key to success. When using a commercial pattern, examine the stitching lines on the pattern. Notice that the line at the top of the opening is shorter than the one at the bottom. Mark accurately so the welt will cover the opening.

5. Complete the welt so that only the lower edge is unfinished. Mark the seamline on the unfinished edge. Trim the seam allowance to 1/4". Topstitch the welt, if desired.

6. With the garment right-side-up, place the welt face down and align the seamline of the welt with the lower edge of the opening. Baste.

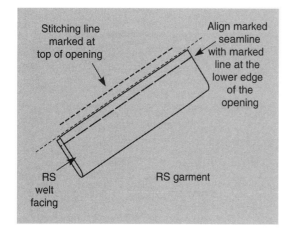

Stitching line marked at top of opening

Align marked seamline with marked line at the lower edge of the opening

RS welt facing

RS garment

Hint: The welt itself is below the opening taking a rest; after all, once it's stitched, it will have to stand up for the rest of its life. Now you know why it's sometimes called a "stand" pocket.

7. Cover the welt with the upper pocket, matching the raw edges. Baste.

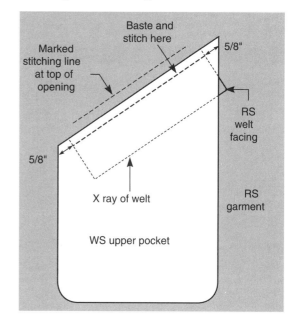

Baste and stitch here

Marked stitching line at top of opening

5/8"

RS welt facing

5/8"

X ray of welt

RS garment

WS upper pocket

Hint: The pocket sack will be two seam allowances wider than the welt.

8. Right sides together, lap the edge of the upper pocket over the stitching line at the top of the pocket opening by 1/4". Turn the work wrong side up. Baste on the stitching line.

9. From the wrong side, stitch the top and bottom of the opening on the basted seamlines. Knot the thread ends.

Hint: Examine your work carefully to be sure the finished welt will cover the top of the opening. If it won't, rip as needed, and stitch again.

10. Slash the opening, and push the pocket sacks through to the wrong side. The welt will flip into place, concealing the opening.

11. Secure the triangles at the ends and complete the pocket bag.

12. If the welt was not topstitched earlier, this is the last opportunity to topstitch the long edge.

13. Sew the ends of the welt in place. (See Welt Applications on page 112.)

14. Steam-press lightly using a self-fabric press cloth.

Variation: Surface Application

Although applied welts are usually sewn into the seamline at the bottom of the opening as previously described, they can be applied to the surface of the garment. This is handy to know if you find, after stitching and slashing, that the welt doesn't cover the opening.

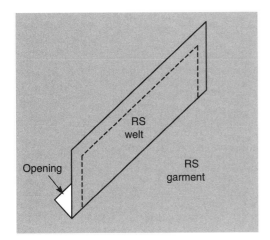

1. Review the directions for the Applied Welt Pockets on page 86 and make these changes.

2. Remove and discard the original welt.

3. Right sides together, baste and stitch the upper pocket to the bottom of the opening.

4. Push the pocket sacks to the wrong side and secure the triangle at the end.

5. Using the original welt pattern, check to be sure it covers the opening. If it doesn't, make the new welt larger or reshape it so it will.

6. Right sides up, position and baste the welt to the garment so it covers the opening. Sew the ends and long edges at the bottom permanently (see Welt Application on page 112).

 Hint: *In haute couture, welts are sometimes finished on all four sides like a patch pocket, then they are sewn to the garment by hand.*

Design Ideas for Single-Welt Pockets

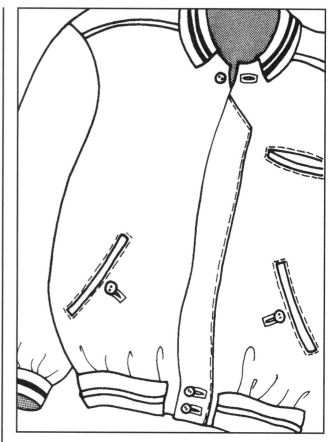

An attractive detail for many fabrics and a variety of designs, single-welt pockets are well-suited for casual utilitarian pockets and elegant cashmere coats.

8. More Slash Pockets

In addition to the basic porthole, double-welt, and single-welt pockets already described, you can create many variations by modifying the basic pockets. Most of the pockets in this section are suitable for double-welt and single-welt pockets, and a few can be used with the porthole pocket.

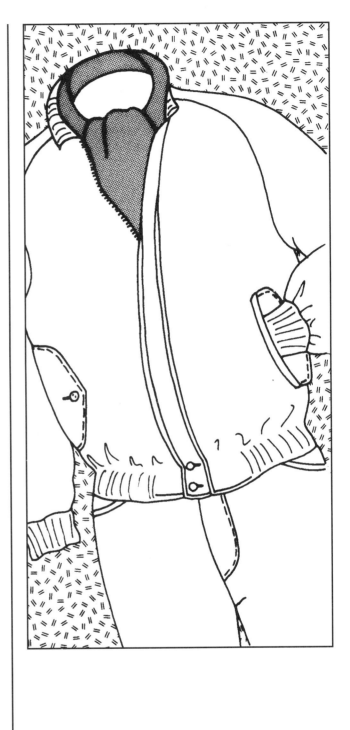

Slash Pocket With a Flap

Design Analysis:

Used on expensive tailored jackets and dresses, the Flap Pocket is easy once you have mastered any of the Strip Methods for double-welt pockets, the Porthole Pocket, or the Set-in Single-Welt Pockets. When used on double welt pockets, the flap can be inserted between the two welts (Method One) or between the upper welt and the garment (Method Two).

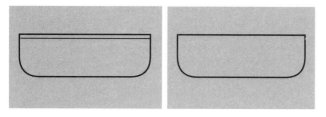

When used on single-welt or porthole pockets, the flap is set-in between the underpocket and the garment. For all of these pockets, the pocket opening doesn't have to be perfect, but the flap must be exactly the right size.

Square, rounded, or angled, the flap design is influenced by the jacket design. The front edge of the flap frequently mirrors the jacket opening, with the back edge more or less parallel to the side seam.

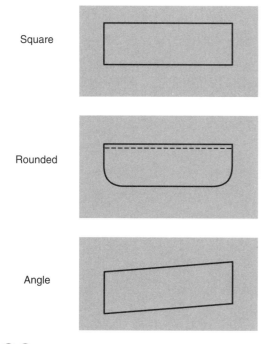

Square

Rounded

Angle

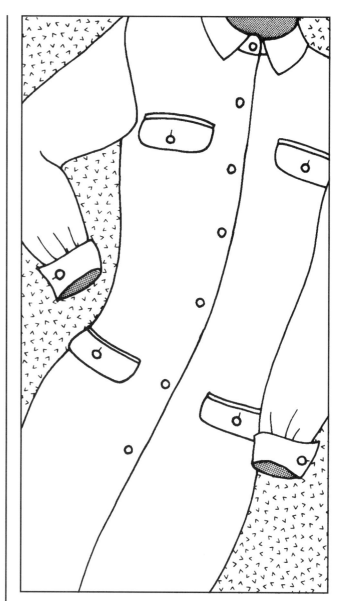

When sewing plaids and stripes, try to avoid designs which have a seam or dart below the pocket so the flap will match the garment at the sides and bottom.

Hint: *On a striped Dior suit designed by Gianfranco Ferré, the pocket flap extended over a seamline. To align the stripes on the flap with the stripes on the garment and shape the flare of the jacket, the pocket flap was seamed at the center.*

Depending on the fabric weight, the flap can be faced with self-fabric or lightweight lining material. It can be topstitched by hand or machine or left plain.

For more information on flaps, see page 114 or *Sew Any Patch Pocket.*

Pattern Development: Method One:

In these directions for a double-welt pocket, the flap is inserted between the two welts. The pocket opening can be made by most methods.

1. Review the directions for the pocket you're making and for flaps.

2. On the completed flap, mark the seamline at the top.

3. On the garment, complete the pocket opening. Baste the welts together and press.

4. Remove the basting which holds the welts together, and insert the flap so the marked seamline at the top of the flap is centered in the opening. Ease the flap in a little more until the marked line is directly under the seamline at the top of the opening. Baste.

Hint: If there are gaps at the end of the opening, the flap is too small. Discard it and make a new one.

5. Turn the garment section wrong side up, and baste the lower welt to the flap facing with a diagonal basting.

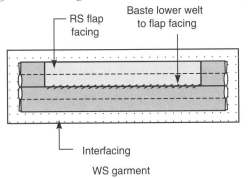

RS flap facing

Baste lower welt to flap facing

Interfacing

WS garment

6. Continuing wrong side up, carefully steam press to remove any ease at the top of the flap.

Hint: Place the flap on a needle board or Velvaboard for pressing. If the flap has ripples after pressing, steam press again right side up, using a press cloth. If the ripples can't be removed, the flap may be too wide. If the flap can't be corrected, make a new flap.

7. Stitch the flap seam allowance to the seamline at the top of the pocket.

8. Complete the pocket.

Method Two:

In these directions the flap is inserted between the upper welt and garment on double-welt pockets, and between the underpocket and garment on porthole and single-welt pockets. On double-welt pockets, a strip method is generally best but the Magic Window can be adapted.

1. Review all directions for the pocket you're making as well as the directions for flaps (see Welts and Flaps on page 106).

2. Make the flap pattern and sew the flaps.

Hint: Flaps are generally finished 1/8" to 1/4" wider than the opening to avoid gaps at the ends. A properly made flap can be tucked into the opening without pulls or puckers.

3. On the garment, stitch the lower welt.

4. On the completed flap, mark the seamline at the top with thread, chalk, or temporary marking pen.

5. Right sides together, align the seamline on the flap with the seamline at the top of the opening, and baste.

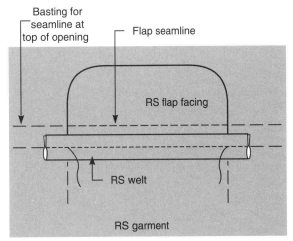

Basting for seamline at top of opening

Flap seamline

RS flap facing

RS welt

RS garment

Hint: On double-welt pockets, trim the seam allowance to 1/4" or the finished width of one welt. Butt the raw edge of the flap to the edge of the lower welt.

6. Place the underpocket or welt on top of the flap and align the seamlines. Baste and stitch permanently.

7. Complete the pocket.

Welt With a Zipper

Design Analysis:

One of the most popular novelty designs, the Welt with a Zipper is also one of the easiest to sew. Used more frequently on double-welt pockets than single-welt pockets, the welt opening is completed first. Depending on the method you're using and your preference, the zipper can be sewn in before or after the pocket sacks are sewn to the opening, but the zipper must be set before the pocket sacks are joined at the sides and bottom.

Sewing Notes:

1. Review all directions for your favorite single-welt or double-welt pocket and make the pocket opening.

2. Before joining the sacks together, center and baste the zipper under the opening with the zipper tab at the top of the opening on vertical pockets and toward the garment center on horizontal or slanted pockets.

Hint: *If you can't purchase a zipper the length you want, use a longer nylon coil zipper. The nylon coil is easier to sew over than a metal zipper. Make a machine or hand bartack to mark the end of the zipper. Trim away the excess zipper below the bartack.*

3. Secure the zipper by hand or machine with ditch-stitching or secure it invisibly by turning the garment back and stitching again on the seamlines at the top and bottom of the opening.

Hints: *I use self-basting zippers which I make by fusing narrow strips of fusible web to the right side of the zipper tape. Then I sew with a zipper foot when setting the zipper.*

If desired, stitch again 1/4" away.

Jacket Lining Pocket

Design Analysis:

Used more frequently on men's jackets than on ladies', the inside coat pocket is located on the lining-side of the garment and generally lies across the facing and lining. On moderate-priced and inexpensive jackets, it is located on the lining on the righthand side. On expensive and custom made jackets, there is a pocket on both right- and left-hand sides and sometimes a third pocket at the waist.

The pocket can be a single-welt or double-welt pocket with or without a button.

Pattern Development:

1. Review all the directions for the pocket you're making.

Hint: Since lining fabrics fray badly, I like the Patch Method (page 70) and finish the pocket with machine ditch-stitching. I also like the one-piece pocket sack and stitch around it twice before trimming the seam to 1/4".

2. Outline the pocket on the lining pattern 1-1/2" to 2-1/2" below the armscye so that it extends 3/4" to 1" into the facing. On women's jackets, locate it nearer the hemline if you prefer, but it should not extend into the hem area.

Draw the finished opening 5-1/2" wide and 1/2" deep. The pocket sack is 8" deep.

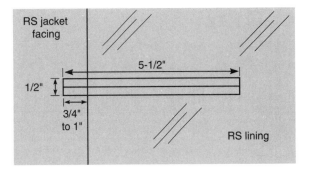

Sewing Notes:

1. Review the Sewing Notes for the pocket you're making.

2. Complete the seam which joins the front facing and the front lining. Press it toward the lining.

3. Interface the garment facing and lining in the pocket area so the pocket won't sag (see page 70), then mark the opening.

Hint: Since many lining fabrics fray badly, I stay the opening with a fusible interfacing even though there may be a slight demarcation line on the lining.

4. Complete the pocket using your favorite method.

Outline Slash Pocket

Design Analysis:

The Outline Slash Pocket, like the Outline Inseam Pocket, can be made with one pocket sack—the underpocket. It can have a double-welt or zipper opening. Marcy Tilton (founder of San Francisco's The Sewing Workshop) likes this pocket for knits because it launders well and it's neat and tidy on the wrong side of unlined garments. It can be modified for a single-welt pocket.

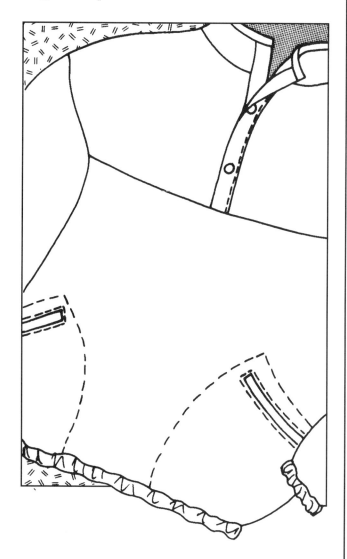

Sewing Notes:

1. Review all directions for the Basic Slash Pocket and the particular pocket you're making.

2. Outline the pocket opening and the stitching line for the pocket sack on the garment pattern.

3. To make the underpocket pattern, trace the stitching line for the pocket sack and add seam allowances to all edges.

Hint: Instead of making a pattern, I just cut a rectangle 2" wider and longer than the finished pocket. After the pocket is stitched, I trim away the excess. If I'm not sure about the stitching outline, I begin with a larger rectangle.

4. Cut the underpocket.

Hint: Synthetic suedes and leathers are a good choice for unlined jackets because they don't ravel.

5. Complete the pocket opening. Press wrong side up.

Hint: When making casual garments, I topstitch around the opening to anchor the welts.

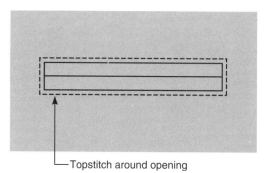

Topstitch around opening

6. Wrong sides up, pin and stitch the underpocket to the seamline at the top of the pocket.

Hint: Use a glue like Sticky Stuff to glue baste the edges of the underpocket temporarily.

7. Turn the garment right side up and topstitch around the sack to secure it. Trim away any excess and press.

Design Ideas for More Slash Pockets

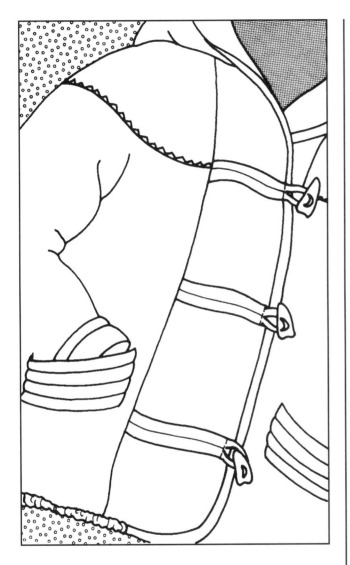

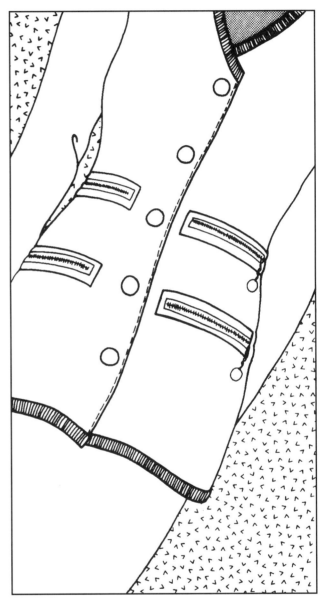

When designing slash pockets, let your imagination run wild and experiment with non-traditional shapes and details. Add a flap, a wide topstitched single welt, or an exposed zipper to create an extraordinary design.

9. Set-in Pockets on a Patch

Many slash pocket designs—welt, bound, and exposed zipper—can be made on patch pockets before the patch pocket is applied to the garment. In addition to creating novelty designs, these pockets allow you to practice your pocket-making skills on small fabric sections with the knowledge that if the pocket isn't perfect you can discard it and cut another. This is a luxury that most of us can't enjoy when the pocket is made on a large garment section.

For perfect patch pockets, review the techniques in my companion book, *Sew Any Patch Pocket.*

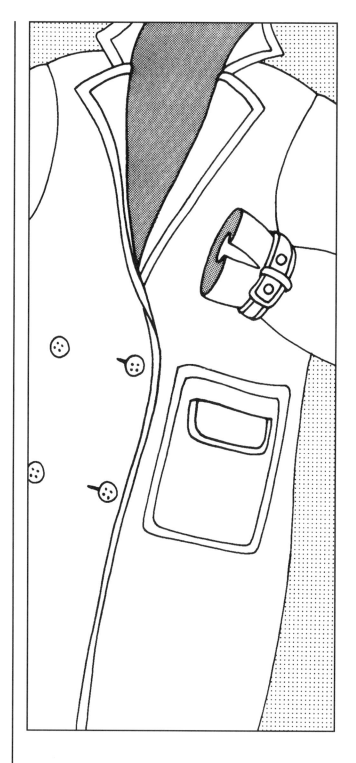

Adele Simpson Pocket

Design Analysis:

Copied from an Adele Simpson dress from the mid-seventies, this pocket was used on a linen A-line skimmer. The design featured a large patch on the right side with a slanted double-welt pocket opening. The patch was completely lined with lining fabric and sewn to the garment at all edges.

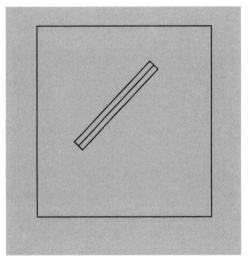

Pattern Development:

These directions are for making a pocket on the right side. Reverse them for making pockets on the left side.

1. Outline the patch and indicate the grainline.

2. Make the finished patch 7" wide by 7-1/2" long and the double welt opening 5-5/8" wide by 1/2" deep.

3. To draw the double-welt opening, first mark point "A" at the pocket top 1/4" from the right corner. Then mark point "B" on the left side 3/4" from the bottom. Connect AB. Mark the opening length on line AB so it is 1-3/4" from A and 2 1/2" from B.

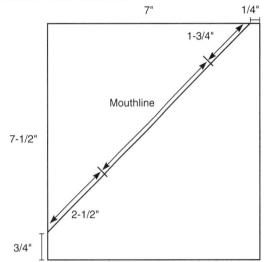

4. Add 1/4" seam allowances to all edges of the patch.

5. Make the pattern for the pocket welts using your favorite method.

Sewing Notes:

1. Review all directions for the Double Welt Pocket you're making.

2. Cut one patch pocket from self-fabric and one from the lining. Cut the welts.

3. Interface the pocket, welts, and the garment under the pocket, as needed.

Hint: Since the pocket opening is on the bias, the interfacing at the opening should be on the straight grain. But, as for most patch pockets, I also interface the entire pocket so it will be sharp and crisp. The welt area can soon get too bulky so I use a very light fusible like Touch o' Gold cut on the lengthwise grain for the welt area.

4. Complete the welt opening.

5. If desired, edgestitch around the pocket opening or stitch a small triangle at each end.

6. Line the pocket. First trim all edges of the lining 1/8", then join the pocket and lining, right sides together. Trim and press. Turn the pocket right side out through the welt opening. Press from the wrong side.

7. Baste an oval around the opening and about 1" from it.

8. Finish the lining opening like a bound buttonhole. Insert a pin in each end of the opening. Then with the lining side up, carefully cut the lining, beginning and ending at the ends. With a small needle and matching thread, begin at the center of the opening. Turn under the raw edge and sew it to the back of the opening, using the point of the needle to shape the ends like a rectangle. Press.

Hint: When finishing the lining, I sew around the opening twice using longer stitches instead of sewing once with tiny stitches.

9. Edgestitch, topstitch, or hand sew the pocket to the garment.

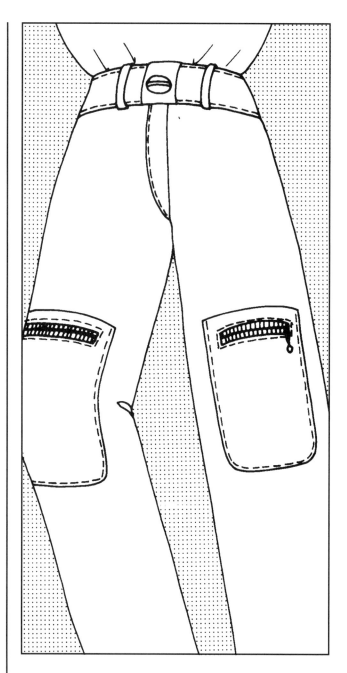

Zippered Welt on a Saddle Bag

Design Analysis:

Particularly nice for cold-weather jackets and fishing vests, this versatile lined pocket can be set like the saddle bag in these directions, or it can be set like a regular patch pocket with the opening at one side or at the top so it forms two separate pockets.

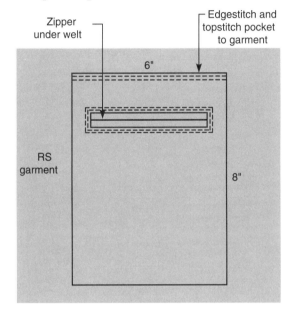

Pattern Development:

Outline the finished patch pocket. Draw the opening for the zipper on the crossgrain 2" from the top. Indicate the grainline on the patch. Add 5/8" seam allowances to all edges.

In these directions, the finished pocket is 6" by 8". The opening is 5" wide by 1/2" deep. The welt opening is located on the crossgrain 2" below the top.

Hint: *The opening can be on any grain, but when it's on the crossgrain or lengthwise grain it's easier to sew.*

Sewing Notes:

1. Review all Sewing Notes for Welt With a Zipper on page 94 and for the welt method you are using.

2. Cut two self-fabric patch pockets. Cut the welts.

Hint: *To reduce bulk when making a double pocket that isn't a saddle bag, cut the patch lining from a lighter weight material.*

3. Interface the pocket, welts, and the pocket area, as needed.

4. Mark the mouthline, complete the opening, and set the zipper.

5. Open the zipper. Right sides together, join the pocket and lining. Trim the seam and press.

6. Turn the pocket right side out. Press.

7. For a saddle bag pocket, edgestitch around the sides and bottom. Pin the pocket in place on the garment and edgestitch the top of the pocket to the garment. Topstitch again 1/4" away.

For a double pocket, edgestitch around the pocket, leaving an opening on one side or at the top.

Easy Zipper Bag

Like the Zippered Welt on a Saddle Bag, the Easy Zipper Bag can be applied as a saddle bag pocket or as a patch pocket. The zipper extends the full width of the pocket and can be set so that it's exposed or covered by one or two welts. The zipper length should not be more than the pocket width to avoid bulk in the seam. On fabrics which don't have a directional pattern, the pocket can be cut all-in-one-piece so the top and bottom of the pocket will be finished with folds instead of seams.

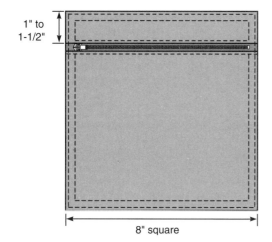

1" to 1-1/2"

8" square

Pattern Development:

This all-in-one pattern is for fabrics which do not have a directional pattern. To make a pattern for a finished pocket 8" square with an exposed zipper, draw a rectangle 9-1/4" wide (the finished pocket width plus two 5/8" seam allowances) and 16" long.

Sewing Notes:

1. Cut one section from the fashion fabric for each pocket.

2. Right sides together, pin the zipper to one short end of the pocket so the zipper is centered. Stitch a 1/4" seam. Pin the other side of the zipper. Check to be sure the top and bottom of the pocket sections are aligned at the zipper. Then stitch.

3. Right sides up, open the zipper and press the pocket away from the zipper. Edgestitch close to the seamlines. Close the zipper. At the end with the zipper pull, baste the ends of the zipper tape together.

4. Right sides together, fold the top of the pocket 1" to 1-1/2" above the zipper. Pin and stitch the side with the basted zipper tape. Open the zipper, then pin and stitch the other side. Trim, grade, and press as needed. Turn the pocket right-side-out and press, using a press cloth as needed.

5. For a saddle bag pocket, edgestitch around the sides and bottom. Pin the pocket in place on the garment and topstitch across the top allowing the pocket to hang free.

Hint: *I usually edgestitch, then topstitch about 1/4" from the edge for more durability.*

For a double pocket, first topstitch the edge of the opening. Then pin the pocket in place on the garment. Topstitch around the pocket, beginning and ending at the opening. Press.

Easy Zipper Variations:

The directions for the Easy Zipper Bag can be adapted for a variety of additional designs. Using your favorite method, set the zipper—with double welts, like a slot zipper or with a single welt at the top like a lapped zipper. Or the raw edges can be bound with narrow bias strips.

When adding double or single welts, add 1-1/4" to the length of the pocket pattern before cutting the fabric. When binding the ends, subtract 1/2" from the pocket pattern length.

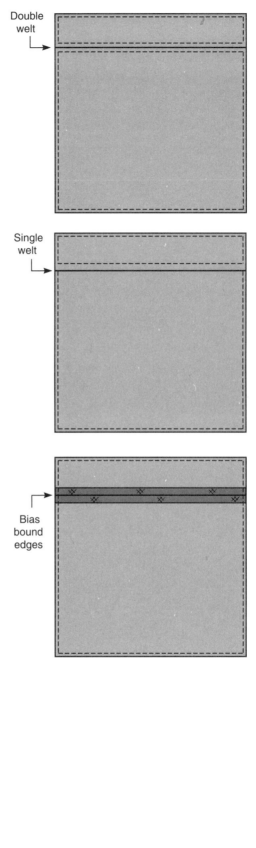

Double welt

Single welt

Bias bound edges

Zippered Porthole on a Saddle Bag

A popular design for outerwear, the Zippered Porthole on a Saddle bag can be made as a single or as a double pocket. The simplest design is a rectangle with an exposed zipper about an inch below the top, but it can be adapted to make a double kangaroo pocket which not only stows your treasures securely but also keeps your hands warm.

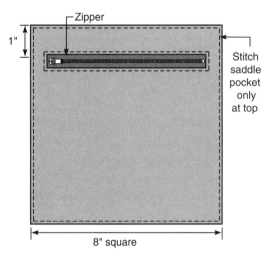

For a double pocket, stitch, leaving all or part of one side open

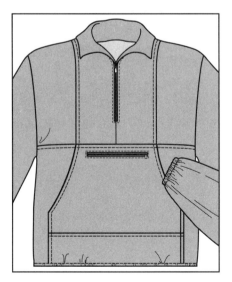

Pattern Development:

In these directions, the finished pocket is 8" square and the opening is about 1" from the top.

1. Outline the pocket so it is an 8" square.

2. Draw a 7" zipper opening about 1" below the top.

3. To make the pocket pattern, add 5/8" seam allowances to all edges.

Sewing Notes:

1. Review all Sewing Notes for the Porthole with a Zipper on page 62.

2. For each pocket, cut two sections from the fashion fabric. One will be the pocket lining.

3. Make the pocket opening on one pocket section. Set the zipper into the opening using your favorite method. Press the opening and topstitch around the zipper.

4. Open the zipper. Right sides together, join the pocket and lining at the edges. Trim, grade, and press as needed. Turn the pocket right side out and press from the under side.

5. For a saddle-bag pocket, topstitch around the sides and bottom. Then pin the pocket in place on the garment and topstitch across the top, allowing the pocket to hang free.

For a double pocket with the opening on the side, topstitch the edge at the opening. Pin the pocket in place on the garment. Topstitch around the pocket, beginning and ending at the opening.

Design Ideas for Pockets on a Patch

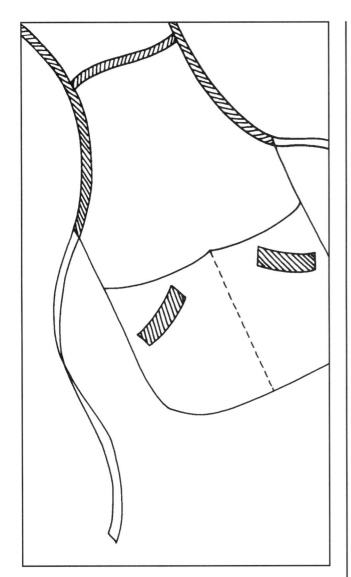

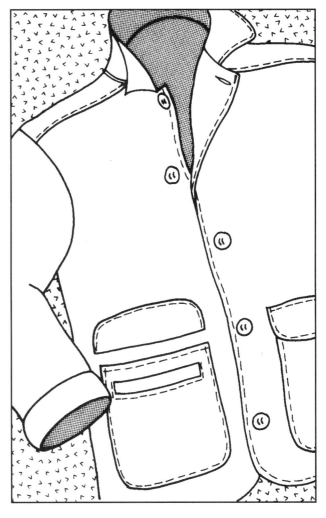

Intimidated by set-in pockets? Have fun and experiment by putting them on a patch.

Appendix:

Welts and Flaps

Set-in welts and flaps can be used with almost any pocket: inseam, slash, or patch. Applied elements which enhance the garment design, they can be decorative fake appendages or utilitarian security covers.

Generally they cover the entire opening. They can be straight or shaped. They are usually faced with a traditional lining material or self-fabric, depending on the fabric weight and garment design. But occasionally they are faced with contrast fabric or hemmed at the free edges. Welts and flaps can also be used without pocket sacks to simulate pockets. Then the false pockets are generally used in pairs.

For perfect welts and flaps, review the techniques in my companion book, *Sew Any Patch Pocket*.

Standards for Welts and Flaps

1. Welts and flaps should be constructed and applied appropriately for the garment design, quality, and use, as well as for the fabric pattern, bulk, weight, transparency, and hand.

2. Welts and flaps should be cut precisely on the indicated grain. They should match the fabric pattern, grain, and nap of the garment section unless designed otherwise. If the entire welt cannot be matched to the fabric pattern, it should match at the edge toward the center or at the bottom. Flaps should match at the edge toward the center or at the top.

3. Straight edges should be straight. Curved corners and edges should be smoothly rounded and flat. Square corners should have well-formed angles and be flat.

4. Seams should be trimmed and graded so that they are inconspicuous and bulk-free.

5. Welts and flaps should be interfaced as needed, so they will maintain their shape. Interfacings, underlinings, and linings should have the same care requirements as the garment.

6. Seamlines should be hidden unless designed otherwise. The facing should not be visible from the right side of the garment.

7. No thread ends or raw edges should be visible.

8. Corners should be reinforced appropriately for the pocket use.

9. Welts and flaps should lie smoothly without pulling, twisting, or sagging when the garment is worn.

10. Topstitching should be appropriate for the design and fabric. It should be evenly stitched from the edges. The length should be appropriate for the fabric, and all stitches should be the same length.

11. Paired welts and flaps should appear identical in size, shape, and placement. They should be equidistant, or look equidistant, from the garment center and be located at the same height.

12. Welts and flaps with trims should be set neatly and appropriately for the design, location, use, and fabric.

Welts

Attached at the bottom and sides like a miniature patch pocket, welts can be sewn into the seam or slash at the pocket opening, or they can be applied to the garment surface just below the pocket opening. The welt is interfaced and assembled using the same criteria and techniques as for the patch pocket, but unlike the patch pocket, it is almost always faced or lined.

Most welts have a straight edge at the top, but the edge can be shaped. Unlike flaps, which generally duplicate the grain of the garment, welts are frequently cut with the grain parallel to the opening. But they can be cut on the bias or lengthwise grain, and, of course, they can duplicate the grain of the garment section.

These directions for welts can be adapted for flaps.

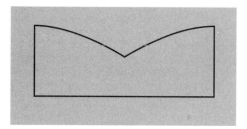

Heart-shaped welt

Pattern Development:

1. Outline the welt on the pattern section. It is frequently a rectangle or parallelogram with the ends parallel to the center front.

Rectangle

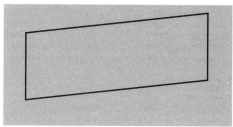

Parallelogram

Hint: On a few designs, I've waited until the garment was almost finished and then I pinned welt shapes on it to determine the size, shape, and location of the pocket. But since the garment is no longer flat, it is much harder to sew the pocket.

2. Indicate the grainline. It can be parallel to the pocket opening or can duplicate the grain of the garment. When the welt will be sewn into a seamline, indicate a matchpoint on the lower edge with a corresponding matchpoint on the seamline at the bottom of the opening.

3. Depending on the garment, welt design, and fabric, decide whether you will make a one-piece welt or a welt with a separate facing.

For *light- to medium-weight fabrics*, the one-piece welt is a good choice.

For *thick or bulky fabrics*, a welt with a separate lining facing is usually flatter.

Trace the welt shape on pattern paper, adding 5/8" seam allowances to all edges. Use the welt pattern to cut the welt and welt facing.

Hint: If the welt has a straight edge at the top, you can make a one-piece welt, which eliminates the seamline and reduces the bulk. To make a one-piece welt, fold the pattern paper horizontally. Align the fold with the seamline at the top of the welt. Trace the cutting lines and grainline. If the welt is slanted, it will have a jog at the foldline.

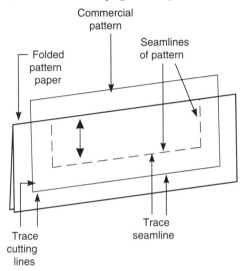

Commercial pattern

Folded pattern paper

Seamlines of pattern

Trace cutting lines

Trace seamline

Sewing Notes:

1. Cut the welt from self-fabric or contrasting fabric, ribbing, or ribbon. Cut the facing from contrast fabric or lining material.

When sewing fabrics with patterns, match the fabric pattern. If the welt is applied over a dart or seamline, match the end toward the garment center.

Hints: To match patterns easily, outline the welt on the fabric with thread or chalk. Lay the welt pattern on the garment section then trace the fabric design onto the welt pattern.

When the design has a pair of welts and the fabric has a pattern, make a pattern for each welt. The fabric pattern is rarely exactly the same.

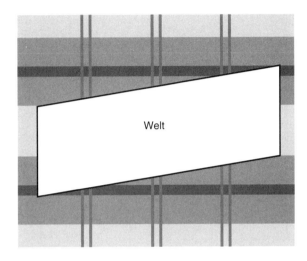

Welt

2. Interface the welt. (See page 111 Sidebar: Interfacing Welts)

Hint: When interfacing welts which do not have a separate facing, do not interface the facing portion of the welt. Generally, fusibles are a good choice. On pockets made from crisp, firmly-woven fabrics, a narrow tape or lightweight selvage at the foldline can sometimes be used instead of interfacing.

3. Face the welt.

Cut the separate welt facing on the same grain as the welt and trim all edges of the welt facing 1/8". Right sides together, match and pin the raw edges of the welt and facing together. Stitch three sides.

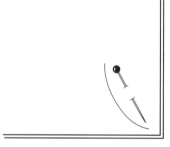

Hints: *Stretch the facing as needed to fit the welt. If the welt has corners, pin a bubble at each corner to control the fullness.*

To avoid rabbit ears at the corners, shorten the stitch length to 20 stitches/inch (1.25mm) and take two stitches across each corner.

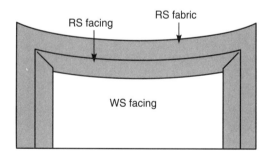

4. Press the welt.

First press the welt flat. Then, for a crisper seamline, press the welt/facing seam allowances in separate directions. Facing side up, press the facing seam allowance toward the facing. Turn the welt over, and press the welt seam allowances toward the welt.

RS facing   RS fabric

WS facing

5. Trim and grade the seam.

Trim the welt seam allowance to 1/4" and trim the facing seam allowance slightly more. On curves, trim with pinking shears or cut out small triangles so the seam will lie flat when the welt is finished.

Hint: *I try to avoid trimming corners because they tend to bunch up when you turn the welt right side out. Instead, I hand sew the seam allowances flat against the interfacing with a couple of stitches.*

6. Turn the welt right side out and press the welt wrong side up. Adjust the facing so the seamline is visible at the edges.

7. Topstitch if desired.

8. Complete the pocket using the directions for that pocket. For decorative fake welts, set the welt to the garment. (See Welt Applications on page 112.)

Interfacing Welts

Welts, like patch pockets, generally need an interfacing to maintain their shape. They can be interfaced with a fusible or sew-in interfacing. It need not be the same interfacing used in other parts of the garment.

Fusible Interfacings

Welts with fusible interfacings have a smoother, sharper appearance than welts with no interfacing. Quick and easy to apply, fusible interfacings are found on ready-to-wear in all price ranges, even on some expensive haute-couture designs.

Some of my favorite fusibles include *Armo Weft, Easy Knit, Fusi-Knit, Knit Fuze, Shapemaker* (woven), *So Sheer, SofBRUSH, SofTOUCH, SofKNIT, Soft 'N Silky, Stacy's Shape-Flex, Suitmaker, Touch O'Gold*, and *Whisper Weft.*

Fusible Application

Cut the interfacing for the welt so that it is the same size as the finished welt or so that it extends into the seam allowances.

1. Select the interfacing.

Hint: *Since welts are small, cut several and experiment with different interfacings. Once you've made your decision, label and file the discards in your interfacing library.*

2. If the interfacing will extend into the seam allowances, use the welt pattern to cut the interfacing. If it won't, cut a new interfacing pattern without seam allowances.

Hint: *Milwaukee teacher Margaret Komives lays the interfacing over the pattern and traces the seamlines with a well-sharpened pencil. Cut out the interfacing, trimming away the pencil line so it won't show through on the garment.*

3. Place the interfacing on the wrong side of the welt, fusible side down, and fuse it in place, using the manufacturer's directions.

Sew-In Interfacings

Traditional sew-in interfacings aren't used as frequently today; however, they are sometimes the perfect choice. Some of my favorite sew-ins include: *Armo Press, Form Flex Woven,* muslin, organza, *Sew-in Durapress, Sewin' Sheer, Poly Supreme, Veri-Shape,* and *Woven Sew-in (Pellon).*

Quick-and-Easy Application

The sew-in interfacing extends into the seam allowances, but since it is stitched into the seamline, a heavy interfacing material is unsuitable.

1. Select the sew-in interfacing.

2. Use the welt pattern to cut the interfacing.

3. Place the interfacing on the wrong side of the welt then stitch the two layers together just inside the seamline.

4. Trim the interfacing close to the stitched line.

A. All-Purpose Welt Application

Applied

These directions are for welts applied to simulate welt pockets, applied welt pockets, and flaps. Appropriate for most fabrics, they can be adapted for the garment quality, fabric, and time available.

The ends of the welt are finished at the outset when the welt is stitched and before it is sewn into the pocket opening. When sewn into the pocket opening, the placement line is marked on the garment at the bottom of the pocket opening.

1. Interface and make the welt, leaving the edge which will be sewn to the garment unfinished.

2. Fold the seam allowances to the facing side or the position the welt will have when it's sewn to the garment. The facing should peek out a little at the raw edge. Pin or baste on the seamline at the bottom of the welt. Trim the seam allowances to 3/8". Remove any pins and press on the foldline.

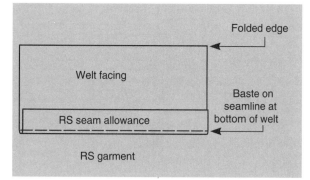

3. With the garment section right side up, place the welt face down so the top of the welt is toward the hemline. Adjust the welt so the raw edges of the welt lap the placement line 1/4". Baste. Stitch 1/4" from the edge. The remaining 1/8" in the seam allowance will be lost in the turn-of-the-cloth.

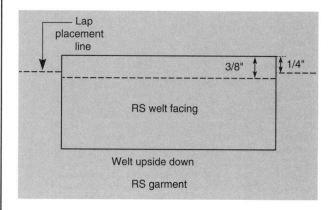

4. Trim the seam to 1/8".

 ***Hint:*** *This is the last opportunity to topstitch the top of the welt without stitching through the garment.*

5. Fold the welt into place. Secure it using one of the following methods.

Topstitch: Topstitching is easy and it encloses all raw edges. It is particularly appropriate when the garment has topstitching at the edges. Topstitch 1/16" and/or 1/4" from the sides of the welt. Secure the thread ends.

"Invisible" stitching: Another easy machine method, this application is a good choice when you don't want the machine stitching to show. Pin the welt in place. Then at one end bubble it slightly to expose the seamline and welt facing. Beginning at the top of the welt, machine or hand stitch on the facing. Secure the thread ends.

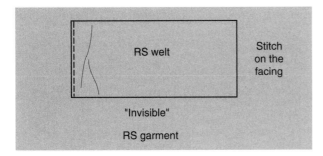

Hint: If you've made the Fake Inside Stitched Patch Pocket on page 34 in Sew Any Patch Pocket, you are already familiar with this technique.

Fell the ends: This hand method is generally used on better garments or welts which have lining facings. Beginning at the foldline, hand sew the ends, using fell stitches.

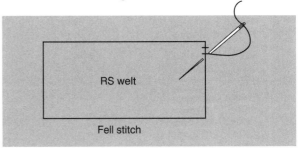

Hint: Avoid pulling the stitches too tight so they won't show.

Catchstitch or running stitch: This application is also used on better garments for an invisible finish. Fold the welt into position then baste about 1/4" from the edges. Turn the garment over. Using the basting as a guide, hand sew with a catchstitch or running stitch through the garment, welt facing, and interfacing.

Hint: Sew carefully to avoid stitches that show on the right side of the welt.

6. Right side up, cover the welt with a press cloth. Press lightly.

B. Welt Application for Lightweight Fabrics

Well-suited for welts on shirtings, washed silk, and other lightweight fabrics, this application is too bulky for medium- and heavy-weight fabrics because the ends of the welt are not finished before the welt is machine-sewn to the garment.

For flatter, more attractive welts, cut a One-Piece Welt with a fold at the top (see page 82), and use a very lightweight interfacing.

1. Interface the welt, but do not assemble the welt before beginning.

2. Wrong sides together, baste the raw edges of the welt together just inside the seamlines.

3. Right sides together, sew the bottom of the welt to the garment using the All-Purpose Application on page 112, beginning and ending 5/8" from the side raw edges. Trim the welt seam to 1/8".

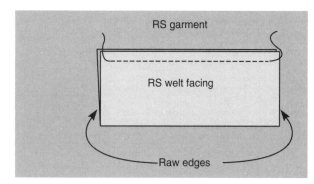

RS garment

RS welt facing

Raw edges

4. Fold the raw edges at the ends under, and trim the seams to 1/4". At the folded edge of the welt, tuck the corner inside the seam allowance. Fold up and pin the welt in place. Edgestitch the ends of the welt

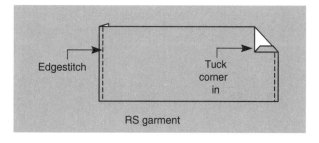

Edgestitch

Tuck corner in

RS garment

Hint: I saw a variation of this technique on a very expensive custom-tailored man's suit and it was used on a real pocket, not a fake. At the ends, the seams were trimmed to a scant 1/4" and secured with fell stitches. Then the corners at the top were folded in. A small prick stitch was used 1/4" from the ends to secure it all and enclose the raw edges.

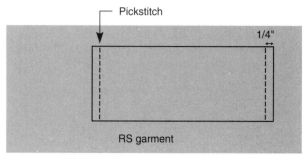

Pickstitch

1/4"

RS garment

Flaps

Called flaps because they hang loose from the upper edge, flaps are generally used in pairs. They can be used alone to simulate slashed pockets or they can be used with inseam, edge, and slashed pockets. When sewn to the front or bottom of an opening, flaps are called cuffs (see page 99, *Sew Any Patch Pocket*). When sewn to the back or top, they are called flaps.

Flaps generally duplicate the nap, grainline, and fabric pattern of the garment section, but they can be cut on the bias or crossgrain. They are usually interfaced and faced, but they can be unlined and hemmed at the free edges. They can be applied by hand or machine.

When sewing flaps, review the previous section on Welts and the directions for the specific pocket you're making.

Design Ideas for Welts and Flaps

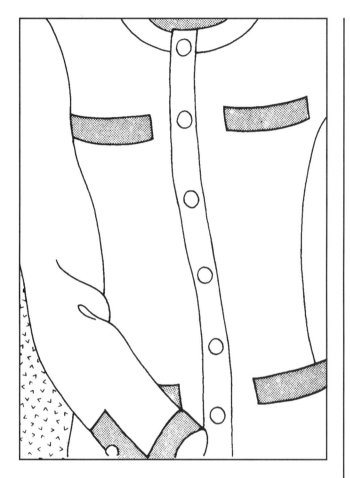

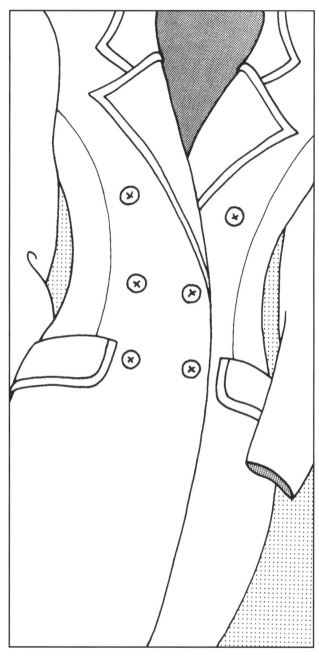

Welts and flaps are often used instead of pockets, but they can also be used to cover, secure, or hide a less-than-perfect opening.

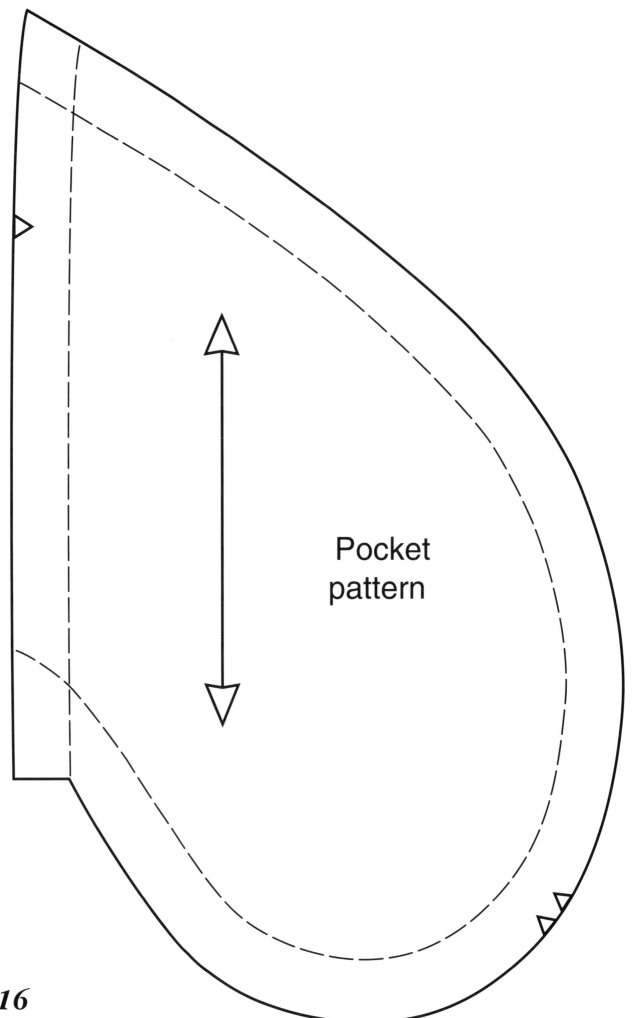

Pocket
pattern

116

Glossary

Backstitch Secure stitching by stitching backwards a few stitches.

Backtack Same as backstitch.

Bartack Satin stitching by stitching backwards a few stitches.

Baste Sew to hold two layers together temporarily.

Bias Fabric cut at 45° angle to lengthwise and crosswise grain.

Binding Fabric used to enclose an edge.

Blindstitch Small V-shaped hemming stitches hidden between the hem and the garment.

Catchstitch Elongated cross-stitches used to hem garments and to secure pocket edges.

Chevron A V-shaped pattern of stripes.

Clapper Wooden tool used in pressing.

Clean finish (1) General term used for seam and hem finishes. (2) A specific edge finish frequently used on the edges of pocket facings to neaten the edge. Sometimes called "turned under and stitched," the edge is first folded under 1/4" – 1/2", then edge stitched.

Clips Short snips cut perpendicular to the edge and into the fabric to make a mark, such as for a pocket opening.

Ditch-stitch Stitch from the right side of the fabric in the well or ditch of the seam.

Edgestitching Topstitching 1/16" from the edge or seamline.

Fabric hand The way the fabric feels and drapes.

Fell stitch Neat, tiny, vertical stitch used on edges.

Foldline The fold at the pocket opening.

Fusible web A weblike adhesive which melts when you apply heat and moisture. Some fusible webs such as *TransFuse* and *Wonder-Under* are applied to paper so they can be ironed onto fabric without sticking to the iron.

Glue-baste To use a glue stick instead of thread to hold fabrics together temporarily.

Grade Reduce the bulk of enclosed seams by trimming the individual seam allowances in different widths, clipping inward curves and corners, notching convex curves, and trimming away excess fabric at outward corners.

Grain The direction the fibers are woven or knit, either lengthwise or crosswise.

Hem allowance The amount of fabric turned to the inside at the pocket opening.

Invisible stitching Stitching on the lining or inside of the pocket in such a way that the stitches aren't visible from the outside.

Matchpoints Drawn lines that intersect a shape and are used to match pocket and garment or lining points exactly.

Nap Short, fuzzy fibers on fabric surface; one-direction designs that must be cut with all pattern pieces laid in the same direction.

Pickstitch A tiny backstitch that doesn't penetrate the lining or facing.

Ravel To fray.

Running stitch Short, permanent hand stitches.

Satin stitch Zigzag stitch of any width with a very short length (.5 or less).

Selvage Finished edges on each side of a woven fabric, running parallel to the lengthwise grain.

Serger A machine that overcasts and trims an edge simultaneously.

Setting a flap (or welt) Applying the flap or welt to the garment.

Slipstitch A hand stitch used to join two layers of fabric from the right side.

Spottack Several stitches made in one place to secure the thread ends.

Styleline The pocket opening. Although it's frequently a straight line, it can be curved.

Taper Make gradually smaller toward the end.

Template A shape made of another substance, such as cardboard or freezer paper, usually the size of the finished pocket.

Temporary marking pen Air- or water-soluble marking pen.

Thread tracing Hand basting used to mark stitching lines and pocket placement.

Toile Test garment made of muslin.

Topstitching Stitching on the right side of the pocket (not necessarily at edge of pocket opening).

Understitch Technique of stitching by hand or machine through the facing and seam allowances.

Index